PUTTING ASSESSMENT INTO ACTION:

Selected Projects from the First Cohort of the Assessment in Action Grant

edited by
Eric Ackermann

Association of College and Research Libraries
A division of the American Library Association
Chicago, Illinois 2015

The paper used in this publication meets the minimum requirements of American National Standard for Information Sciences–Permanence of Paper for Printed Library Materials, ANSI Z39.48-1992. ∞

Library of Congress Cataloging-in-Publication Data

Names: Ackermann, Eric, editor.
Title: Putting assessment into action : selected projects from the first
  cohort of the Assessment in Action grant / edited by Eric Ackermann.
Description: Chicago : Association of College and Research Libraries, a
  division of the American Library Association, 2015. | Includes
  bibliographical references.
Identifiers: LCCN 2015043293 (print) | LCCN 2015048482 (ebook) | ISBN
  9780838988138 (pbk.) | ISBN 9780838988145 (PDF) | ISBN 9780838988152
  (ePub) | ISBN 9780838988169 (Kindle) | ISBN 9780838988145 (pdf) | ISBN
  9780838988152 (epub) | ISBN 9780838988169 (kindle) | ISBN 9780838988138
  (paperback)
Subjects: LCSH: Academic libraries--United States--Evaluation--Case studies.
  | Academic libraries--Canada--Evaluation--Case studies. | Information
  literacy--Study and teaching (Higher)--Evaluation--Case studies. |
  Academic libraries--Relations with faculty and curriculum.
Classification: LCC Z675.U5 P895 2015 (print) | LCC Z675.U5 (ebook) | DDC
  027.70973--dc23
LC record available at http://lccn.loc.gov/2015043293

Printed in the United States of America.

19 18 17 16 15 5 4 3 2 1

Table of Contents

Part 1: Assessing Information Literacy/Library Instruction

First Year Students/First Year Experience

Second to Fourth Year Undergraduates

Graduate Students

Institutional

Part 2: Assessing Outreach, Services and Spaces

Outreach

Services

Spaces

Part 3: Longitudinal Assessment

Foreword

Purpose

Library assessment is still relatively new, and is poised to grow rapidly after the completion of the Assessment in Action (AiA) grant.[1] Even so, many librarians will be new to their assessment responsibilities, which will involve creating and implementing assessment projects. This casebook is designed to help them to approach the question of selecting the best, most effective assessment methods for the activity or program they wish to assess. It does not require one to have an extensive previous knowledge of the available assessment methodologies, research designs, or statistics in order to determine which one (or more) will work best for their project. Unlike many books on this subject, this one allows the selection of appropriate assessment method(s) based on the activity or program being assessed rather than the specifics of a particular research design, method, or statistical protocol.

Organization

The twenty-seven chapters in this casebook are based on selected projects created and implemented by the teams selected to participate in the first cohort of the AiA grant.[2] Each chapter is focused on a separate project, and addresses various assessment method and process issues that were confronted by its author(s) during the course of planning and executing their chosen project. Although some of these methodological issues were discussed in the posters created from these projects and presented at 2014 ALA Annual Conference,[3] the author(s) discusses them in greater depth and detail. In particular, each chapter addresses the following topics:

- How did you choose the method(s) used in your project?

- How well did the project's method(s) relate to (or operationalize) your project's inquiry question?
- What limitations did you encounter when using your method(s)?
- Did you recruit anyone outside the library to help you implement the project's method(s)?
- Do you have any suggestions for others thinking about using the same method(s)?

Can you recommend any alternative method(s) for use when exploring a similar inquiry question?

Scope and Limits

This casebook is intended to complement currently available resource produced as part of the Assessment in Action grant[4] and ACRL's Value of Academic Libraries initiative.[5] It is limited by size considerations to a sample of twenty-seven of the seventy-four projects produced by the first cohort during 2013–14. The scope of the book reflects the diversity of the cohort's project types (what is being assessed) and home institutions (research universities to community colleges). The bulk of the chapters (17 or 63%) are concerned with projects that assess various aspects of information literacy/library instruction. Seven (or 26%) of the chapters concern projects assessing library outreach, services, or spaces; while the remaining three chapters (or 11%) involve longitudinal assessment projects. The authors represent twenty-five American and two Canadian institutions, comprising ten (or 37%) Master's Colleges & Universities, six (or 22%) Doctoral/Research Universities, six (or 22%) Research Universities, three (or 11%) Baccalaureate Colleges, one Tribal (or 4%), and one (or 4%) Associate (i.e., Community College).[6]

Acknowledgments

I would like to take a moment to acknowledge and thank the people who made this casebook possible. Kara Malenfant, Senior Strategist for Special Initiatives at the Association of College and Research Libraries (ACRL) for recruiting (and encouraging) me to be the editor, as well as guiding the focus of the book. Kathryn Deiss, Content Strategist at ACRL for successfully shepherding it (and us) through publication process. Most importantly

I wish to thank all my first cohort colleagues who agreed to participate as chapter authors in this endeavor. Without their commitment and hard work this book would not exist.

Eric Ackermann, Editor
McConnell Library, Radford University
October 15, 2015

Notes

1. For more information about the AiA grant, and a list of the participating institutions, see Association of College and Research Libraries, "AiA Overview," Assessment in Action: Academic Libraries and Student Success, http://www.ala.org/acrl/AiA (accessed October 10, 2015); and Karen Brown and Kara J. Malenfant, *Academic Library Contributions to Student Success: Documented Practices from the Field* (Chicago, IL: Association of College and Research Libraries, 2015), http://www.ala.org/acrl/sites/ala.org.acrl/files/content/issues/value/contributions_report.pdf (accessed October 11, 2015), 1.
2. For more information about the first cohort teams, see Brown & Malenfant, *Library Contributions to Student Success*, 5–6.
3. The abstracts of these posters are available at http://www.acrl.ala.org/value/wp-content/uploads/2014/06/AiA-poster-guide-ALA-AC-2014.pdf
4. For example, Brown & Malenfant, *Library Contributions to Student Success*; and Association of College and Research Libraries, "Program Summaries and Reports," Assessment in Action: Academic Libraries and Student Success, http://www.ala.org/acrl/AiA (accessed October 10, 2015).
5. For example, Megan Oakleaf, *Value of Academic Libraries: A Comprehensive Research Review and Report* (Chicago, IL: Association of College and Research Libraries, 2010), http://www.ala.org/ala/mgrps/divs/acrl/issues/value/val_report.pdf (accessed August 16, 2015); and Douglas Cook and Lesley Farmer, eds., *Using Qualitative Methods in Action Research: How Librarians Can Get to the Why of Data* (Chicago, IL: Association of College and Research Libraries, 2011), http://www.alastore.ala.org/detail.aspx?ID=3394 (accessed September 21, 2015)
6. Association of College and Research Libraries, "Search," Assessment in Action, http://apply.ala.org/aia/public (accessed October 12, 2015).

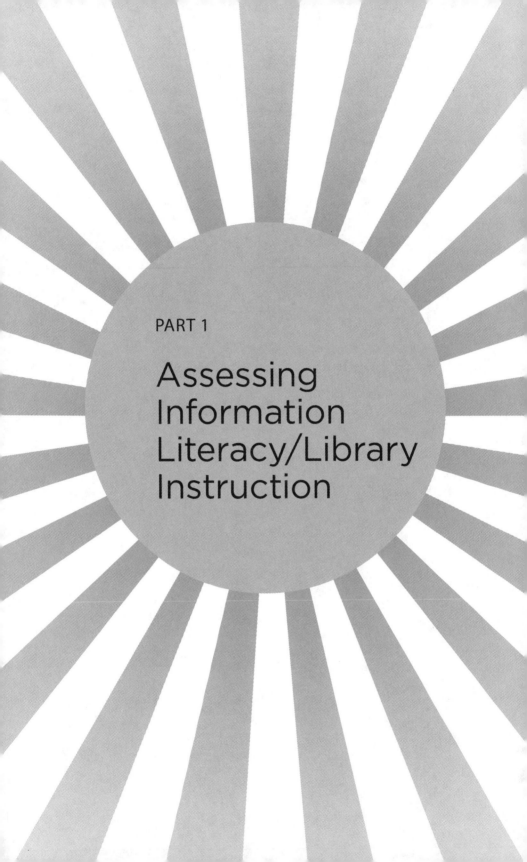

PART 1

Assessing Information Literacy/Library Instruction

CHAPTER 1

"I Felt Like Such a Freshman:"

Reflections on DePaul University Library's Assessment in Action Project

Heather Jagman

DePaul University
hjagman@depaul.edu

DEPAUL UNIVERSITY IS A diverse, urban, Catholic institution located in Chicago, Illinois. The University is committed to the city, and encourages faculty and students to think of Chicago as an extension of their classroom and learning community. Exposure to the city and urban life begins immediately after students arrive on campus; all incoming first year students are required to enroll in either Discover Chicago or Explore Chicago, a "First Year Experience" course also known as the "Chicago Quarter." As the names imply, these classes focus on some aspect of life in Chicago and provide students with an opportunity to experience the city through field visits to different neighborhoods. Classes tour a variety of places from cemeteries and science labs to ethnic grocery stores and museums. The city becomes a laboratory for classes to explore a variety of topics and issues through the disciplinary lens of the faculty instructor. These courses are team-led. Each team consists of a faculty instructor, a staff professional, and student mentor. In addition to this academic component, the

Chicago Quarter also includes a "Common Hour," led by a student mentor with assistance from the staff professional. The Common Hour provides peer support while introducing students to a variety of topics designed to support student success, such as understanding diversity, financial literacy, wellness and academic success skills. In addition to having the support of the staff professional and faculty member, the student mentors are required to enroll in a series of classes introducing them to peer education theory and practice. These courses provide the mentors with information on college student development as well as a peer support network of their own. Student Affairs staff from our Office of New Student and Family Engagement provide the curriculum and instruction for these courses.

In 2013 I worked with colleagues from DePaul's Writing Center, Academic Advising, New Student and Family Engagement, and the Center for Students with Disabilities to design a Common Hour lesson plan and associated library assignment to be delivered and graded by Chicago Quarter student mentors as part of the Discover/ Explore Chicago curriculum. As co-curricular units charged with supporting student success, we wanted to design a lesson plan that would increase students' confidence and sense of belonging as well as cultivate certain habits of mind, like being curious and seeking expertise. Our hope was to build students' identity as scholars, and address their anxiety regarding new spaces and experiences. We also needed to replace an outmoded and very didactic library assignment focused more on where to click than how to think.

Our new assignment combined action and reflection. We asked students to consider a topic of personal or academic interest, use the library discovery tool to identify an item in our holdings, physically find the item in the library, check it out, and afterward respond to a series of reflection questions in the form of a brief essay to be graded by the peer mentors. We intentionally left out any instructions on searching (or even locating) the online library catalog. We wanted students to experiment, try searching on their own—possibly not get things exactly right at first—and learn from the experience. One of the hopes of the original assignment was that it would also increase students' confidence and sense of belonging by giving them a chance to get out of their comfort zones, perhaps struggle a bit, but see that they would eventually be able to succeed. In reflecting on their success, students would then articulate to themselves that they can be persistent and successful.

In 2013 when we conducted this assessment, 33% of DePaul's first year students were first generation college students, and neither parent had a college degree. Stacy Brinkman, Katie Gibson, and Jenny Presnell note that first-generation students perceive themselves as being outsiders, and reported that this feeling created stress, because they "simply assumed that the library was one more instance of academic cluelessness."[1] Supporting first generation college students is a critical component of DePaul's mission, and the Library wants to foster an environment that helps these students succeed.

Academic libraries can be intimidating to many students—it's not just first generation students who struggle. Project Information Literacy reports that in general, first year students feel overwhelmed by college level research assignments and are intimidated by the amount of information they are dealing with for the first time.[2] Getting students 'over themselves' and into the physical library can facilitate student retention and success. Furthermore, research from the University of Minnesota suggests that first year students who use the library at least once during their first semester have higher grade point averages than their peers, and are more likely to persist into the next semester.[3]

In addition to completing a physical task, students in our program reflected on that experience in the form of a brief essay. Reflection papers are an increasingly popular assignment at DePaul. Like making use of library resources, writing a reflection paper might be something students would be expected to do prior to formal library instruction in their first year writing program. Mary Ryan argues that active reflection on such activities helps people to understand the context of their learning and use this knowledge "to re-imagine and ultimately improve future experience."[4]

Creating the Assignment

Creating an assignment that combined action and reflection presented a number of opportunities and challenges. We had to think carefully about what we wanted students to address in their reflection papers. Would we be able to tell from their responses how the library contributes to their success? What could we, as a team, learn about how the library contributes to student learning and engagement? It helped us to first consider our learning objectives, and then create our assignment. It was helpful to be very explicit in our instructions to the students. We found that if you ask students to explain how the library "supports their success as academic learners," they will do their best to tell you.

Asking students to comment on their library experiences in the form of a reflection essay (guided by our questions) provided us with an authentic and direct measure of whether (and how) they learned to find what they were looking for, what they noticed about our library, and how they felt about it. Not only was this interesting for us as researchers, but we also found that the act of writing a reflective response seemed to provide an additional, metacognitive experience for the students. Our assignment gave students an experience, and an opportunity to reflect on that experience, and plan for future success. (In our analysis, we noticed a number of students articulated their plans to use library materials and services in the future.)

The assignment was designed to be distributed and graded by a peer mentor. Because students were writing for their peers, we felt these new student voices and concerns were likely more authentic than they would have been had they been writing for a librarian. Students did not know until they were offered the opportunity to participate in our study that a research team was interested in what they had to say. However, because our research team was not connected to these students or classes directly, we had to make special arrangements and work with our local Institutional Review Board in order to collect and analyze the student artifacts. Our study was granted an exemption. The student essays would be anonymized prior to reaching us, so we would have no way of identifying the students. Our lack of direct connection to these students presented another problem. How could we encourage the peer mentors to help us by recruiting their Common Hour students to participate? We had no relationship with them. Prior to applying to the Assessment in Action (AiA) project, our team had consisted of representatives from our co-curricular units. However, we realized that in order for our AiA project to work well, we would need to invite someone from the Office of New Student and Family Engagement (NSFE) to join our team. NSFE staff were able to recruit peer mentors who in turn would recruit their students to participate during the weekly meetings of their Peer Education Theory and Practice classes.

Methodology

We decided to assess the student essays by applying a rubric focused on four outcomes based on the Association of American Colleges and Universities VALUE rubric for Information Literacy[5]:

- Students will visit the DePaul University libraries and gain familiarity with the physical attributes of the libraries.
- Students will complete a successful search for material and check out at least one item.
- Students will identify and articulate novel features of the academic library relative to their prior experience with libraries.
- Students will articulate at least one way the library can support their success as university learners.

Deciding on definitions that would enable us to rank each outcome from 1 to 4 wasn't as easy as we thought it. Not every outcome authentically lent itself to four discrete levels of achievement. We may have made things more complicated than necessary, but this was out first time attempting such an assessment, and we wanted to make sure that we had plenty of options. Looking back, I would recommend focusing on assessing just one or two outcomes at a time. If you are interested in assessing multiple outcomes, consider creating an assessment cycle that allows you to rotate through outcomes on a regular basis.

Establishing Inter-Rater Agreement

Since our AiA team worked together to write the assignment and develop the rubric, one might think establishing inter-rater reliability would be a snap, but it was not without challenges. As we read the essays, we needed to regularly remind ourselves that we could only rate the evidence that students provided. It is possible that some students actually succeeded (or failed), but were not very good at communicating their experience in writing. Enlisting non-librarians to read and rate the reflection essays was enlightening, and it also illuminated how differently things can look to us through our "librarian-eyes." My colleagues did not always recognize when a student described something that was more or less a library impossibility (like a student reporting that they found a book about flute and flute playing in the 815's) and rated the student's performance quite differently than I did. We worked to establish inter-rater agreement by reading seven essays together and then discussing our ratings and adjusting our definitions (and even the rubric) accordingly. Team members then read and rated twenty-five essays on their own. I read the entire collection of ninety-seven essays, and then met with each rater to discuss our ratings and come to consensus. I don't think this would have been possible if we'd had any more essays or if the essays had been much longer than one or two pages.

Furthermore, reading the entire collection of essays provided me with an opportunity to observe patterns and consider how we might apply alternate methods of analysis in the future. Employing the rubric allowed us to demonstrate that students were able to succeed and to what degree[6], but it did not give us any way to describe the students' learning processes. Our interest in understanding student behavior ultimately led to another research project in which a colleague and I used Nvivo Qualitative Analysis software to code the text and look for patterns in how students approached the library, overcame hurdles and described their emotional state. The ability to extract quotes from the essays in a meaningful way makes it easier to tell your story to your stakeholders.

Notes

1. Stacy Brinkman, Katie Gibson, and Jenny Presnell, "When the Helicopters Are Silent: The Information Seeking Strategies of First-Generation College Students," paper presented at the Association of College and Research Libraries Conference, Indianapolis, IN, April 2013, accessed November 22, 2014, http://www.ala.org/acrl/sites/ala.org.acrl/files/content/conferences/confsandpreconfs/2013/papers/BrinkmanGibsonPresnell_When.pdf

2. Alison J. Head, "Learning the Ropes: How Freshmen Conduct Course Research Once They Enter College" (Project Information Literacy, December 4, 2013), accessed March 4, 2014, http://projectinfolit.org/images/pdfs/pil_2013_freshmenstudy_fullreport.pdf

3. Krista M. Soria, Jan Fransen and Shane Nackerud, "Library Use and Undergraduate Student Outcomes: New Evidence for Students' Retention and Academic Success," *portal: Libraries & the Academy*, 13, no. 2 (2013): 147–164.

4. Mary Ryan, "Conceptualizing and Teaching Discursive and Performative Reflection in Higher Education," *Studies in Continuing Education* 34, no. 2 (October 7, 2011): 209, doi:10.1080/0158037X.2011.611799

5. "Information Literacy VALUE Rubric," Association of American Colleges and Universities, 2010, accessed July 10, 2013, http://www.aacu.org/value/rubrics/information-literacy

6. For more information about our findings, see Heather Jagman, Lisa Davidson, Lauri Dietz, Jodi Faulk, and Antonietta Fitzpatrick, " 'I Felt like Such a Freshman': Creating Library Insiders," accessed June 25, 2015, http://works.bepress.com/heather_jagman/7

CHAPTER 2

Honor Bound:

Assessing Library Interventions into the Complex Problem of Academic Integrity

Jacalyn A. Kremer

DiMenna-Nyselius Library, Fairfield University
jkremer@fairfield.edu

ALIGNED WITH FAIRFIELD UNIVERSITY'S mission to foster student commitment to academic excellence and a sense of social responsibility, the DiMenna-Nyselius Library began a serious exploration of academic integrity in the Fall 2009. The Library has been actively involved since then with Fairfield University's academic integrity initiatives, resulting in the Library's recognition as a leading campus resource on academic integrity. The Library's work is motivated by the belief that academic libraries can be a major contributor to solving the complex problem of academic dishonesty by educating faculty and students through workshops, information literacy classes, and student learning modules. These education efforts focused on issues such as avoiding plagiarism, citing sources and the interdependent responsibilities of both students and faculty. (You can see more details of the DiMenna-Nyselius Library's academic integrity work at http://librarybestbets.fairfield.edu/academicintegrity/.)

As part of the DiMenna-Nyselius Library's academic integrity efforts, our librarians developed and implemented two direct instruction modules for first-year students delivered through Fairfield University's First-Year Experience program:

- **Module 1:** An academic integrity classroom lesson integrated into the First-Year Experience program consisting of assigned readings, guided discussion questions on the readings, classroom activities and a writing prompt assigned for homework.
- **Module 2:** A web-based tutorial *Avoiding Plagiarism Tutorial* designed to educate students about citation rules, tips for avoiding plagiarism, Fairfield University's Honor Code and academic integrity.

Prior to the Assessment in Action (AiA) grant, no formal assessment of the impact of these direct instruction modules on student learning had been undertaken. Our AiA project focused on the assessment of these two instruction modules, with specific emphasis on quantifying their impact on (a) students' understanding of academic integrity, and (b) students' skills for integrating and citing sources in ways that avoid plagiarism.

Partnerships

Since the modules are incorporated into the First Year Experience program, it was vital we include the head of the First Year Experience program on our assessment team. As part of the team, the head of the First Year Experience program was instrumental in coordinating the delivery of the lessons and administering the assessment. Since citing sources and avoiding plagiarism encompass multi-faceted, higher order skills, we invited Fairfield University's Writing Center Director (and an expert on student writing issues) to be part of the team. We also wanted the assessment project to be viewed not only as a library initiative, but also as a contribution to the University's assessment plans and its understanding of its students. Therefore the participation of Associate V-President of Academic Affairs and Assessment in the team placed our work within the larger University's assessment initiatives. All three of these colleagues took part in the Assessment in Action training, participated in the scoring of the assessments and in the compilation of results. Having participation from experts across campus and with differing expertise added great value to the project, linking all of our work together by its impact on student learning and institutional mission.

Assessing Complex Learning

Academic integrity is the cornerstone of learning. While highly valued at every higher education institution, educators do not have universal agreement on the skills and mindsets that make up a person of academic integrity. It is a highly complex concept that defies a check list approach. This complexities led us to question how and even if academic integrity can be assessed. How do we assess the intangible? Can academic integrity be quantified? It is easy to get stymied. We decided that to fully assess this intangible of academic integrity may not be possible, but we can get indications of progress towards achieving this goal of academic integrity.[1]

Module 1: Academic Integrity Lesson

The *Academic Integrity Lesson* learning module developed by our librarians and integrated into all First-Year Experience classes consisted of two assigned readings: *Integrity: Academic and Political. A Letter to My Students* [2] and the Fairfield University Honor Code. It also included corresponding guided discussion questions and group classroom activities. (To see the complete learning module, go to http://librarybest-bets.fairfield.edu/academicintegrity/firstyear.) The purpose of the lesson was to discuss and reflect upon issues related to academic integrity in order to promote a University culture of "honesty, trust, fairness, responsibility and courage."[3] The measurement of an intangible University culture of academic integrity was vexing. A meeting with our Director of Institutional Research was particularly helpful in offering these two tips: 1) it is best to use agreed-upon and accepted standards and tools in higher education, and 2) the establishment of clear learning outcomes is essential.

The team felt the American Association of Colleges and Universities' VALUE (Valid Assessment of Learning in Undergraduate Education) project was an excellent starting point, offering accepted standards and tools. VALUE is a campus-based assessment initiative sponsored by American Association of Colleges and Universities as part of its LEAP initiative that offers 16 rubrics to assess students' own authentic work.[4] Notably, the American Association of Colleges and Universities' Ethical Reasoning Rubric from VALUE addresses the difficulties in attempting to assess the sometimes fluid concept of academic integrity. It points out that "pragmatically it would be difficult, if not impossible, to judge whether or not students would act ethically when faced with real ethical situations. What can be evaluated using a rubric is whether students have the intellectual tools to make ethical choices."[5] The VALUE rubrics were a key starting point to clarify our thinking and led our assessment team to consensus on using a rubric tool to assess student learning from the lesson.

Additionally, the selection of a rubric tool as the appropriate method was supported by its recognition as valuable in evaluating subjective work that ranges across a continuum.[6] A well designed rubric when applied to student work takes subjective judgments and turns them into objective assessments using quantitative scales. We chose a descriptive rubric format. A descriptive rubric has three components: 1) the learning outcomes to be assessed (usually in the first column), 2) the levels of performance (usually numbers across the top row) and 3) the definitions of the quality of the performance (the inside of the table).[7] While rubrics can be holist or analytic, we chose an analytic rubric that allowed us to examine and assess individual learning outcomes.[8]

The determination of the authentic student work to be assessed flowed from the choice of the descriptive rubric assessment tool. To state this another way, the assessment method came first and then we decided on the type of work to be assessed. The student work assigned was a reflection essay. Our assessment methodology then became an exploratory essay review approach where we looked at a representative sample of essays. This representative sample of 10% of the approximately 950 essays was generated by our Director of Institutional Research, and mirrored the demographics of the larger first-year student population.

A well designed rubric is predicated on clear learning objectives. The development of learning objectives is both intellectual challenging and time consuming. Most important to crafting the learning objectives is to state specific outcomes that can then be assessed. In the learning outcomes developed by the assessment team, clear outcomes are stated and can be demonstrated. See the example below, with use of action verbs such as **IDENTIFY, EXPLAIN** and **PROBLEM-SOLVE**.

    Learning Objective # 1: First–year students **IDENTIFY** and **EXPLAIN** their academic responsibilities as members of the Fairfield University community.

Learning Objective # 2: First-year students **IDENTIFY** their own behaviors that could contribute to Academic Integrity violations and **PROBLEM-SOLVE** how to act responsibly in their scholarly community.

Once the learning objectives were done, we created a *draft* rubric that quantified the outcomes of the learning objectives with score ranges on a continuum. The draft rubric was then put through a norming process where the team independently tested the rubric using actual essays. The results were then compared through group discussions and changes were made to the rubric. This norming process is vital to creating a well-designed rubric. For those considering developing a rubric, we recommend allotting significant amounts of time for the norming process. Also, we found it was important that everyone participating in the assessment be part of the entire norming process. The group discussions that occur during the norming helps reduce ambiguity during scoring and ultimately saves time and improves confidence in the results.

The team wanted all first-years to go through the lesson and therefore we did not have a control group to use for comparison. To remedy this problem, we used a waiting control group approach. In our case this meant we waited to give 1/2 the group the lesson until *after* both groups had written the essay. So we were able to compare essays from one group who had the lesson to the other group who did not have the lesson.

Module 2: *Avoiding Plagiarism Tutorial*

The online *Avoiding Plagiarism Tutorial* currently being taken by first-years was heavily based on our previous tutorial *Plagiarism Court*, a 2002 PRIMO winner. We knew it needed significant updates and wanted an assessment method that would not only tell us what our first-year students know about plagiarism but would also help us to shape the new plagiarism tutorial. The online tutorial presented information including:

1. Defining plagiarism.
2. Tips on how to avoid plagiarism, such as note taking and paraphrasing.
3. Why citing is important.
4. Specific rules on how to do citations.

This information was displayed in a sequential non-interactive format, followed by a 15 question multiple choice question.

While for some plagiarism is a black and white issue, for many in academia plagiarism is the grayest of areas. What is considered common knowledge by one faculty member is not common to another. What one defines as cheating or copying, another sees as a mistake or a lack of understanding about citations. Plagiarism is "a multi-faceted and ethically complex problem."[9] The library's approach in the plagiarism tutorial is to educate about why we cite, with the idea that "knowing how to understand and synthesize complex, lengthy sources is essential to effective plagiarism prevention."[10] Avoiding plagiarism requires a developed set of higher-order skills and knowledge. Again, we came back to our concern on the difficulty of assessing highly complex learning. We are not alone in our concerns as a survey of high-quality plagiarism tutorials employed by academic libraries shows that 56% collect no data at all on its effectiveness.[11] We concluded no one assessment tool could capture the knowledge about plagiarism and citing rules as well as assess if students were able to apply their knowledge in their own writing. Therefore, our original idea was to split the assessment of the plagiarism tutorial into two parts:

1. **Knowledge:** Do students know the definition of plagiarism? Can students recognize examples of proper paraphrasing? Do students know the basic rules of citation?

2. **Skills:** In an authentic writing assignment, can students demonstrate proper citation techniques? Can they avoid patchwork writing? Can they properly paraphrase?

It became apparent that what amounted to two different assessment projects on the plagiarism tutorial effectiveness was not feasible due to time requirements. It is important to acknowledge here that decisions regarding assessment must be based on practicalities of our own work loads, what is feasible technologically and what we ultimately want to learn from assessment. In that vein, we decided to assess the knowledge portion only because it was less time consuming, could be done with electronic scoring and it would give us more concrete information about the effectiveness of the plagiarism tutorial. Once we decided to assess the knowledge portion, we chose a multiple choice quiz as our assessment method as they are well-suited for testing the recall of knowledge.

Approximately 950 first-year students take the plagiarism tutorial every year. If we wanted to assess the effectiveness of it we could either pick a representative sample or find a way to score all of the students electronically. The grading options in Blackboard include a multiple choice quiz. We decided to move the tutorial into Blackboard, enroll all 950 students into it, and use the grading system in Blackboard to administer and automatically grade the multiple choice quiz. Blackboard allowed us to easily monitor who had and who had not taken the tutorial. The grading options in Blackboard made it the practical choice.

Our next step was to identify the learning objectives of the tutorial. In a recent survey, only 16% of library designed plagiarism tutorials had measurable learning objectives. This is especially problematic as without these objectives, quiz questions do not accurately gauge learning.[12] We crafted six learning objectives for the plagiarism tutorial. The crafting of the learning objectives was done collaboratively by the librarian and the Associate Vice-President of Academic Affairs and Assessment. We highly recommend getting input from at least one other person when crafting learning objectives.

After crafting the six learning objectives, we set criteria that define the acceptable performance for each learning objective. These criteria allowed us to know when we have been successful and when we have not. The next step of writing the multiple choice question that corresponds to the criteria is time consuming and requires a great deal of skill and experience. We repeatedly had to remind ourselves that for each question there should be only one correct or best answer. The other choices should be foils, but foils that seem plausible. In total, we decided to have four choices to choose from, which is fairly standard. One advantage of running a multiple choice quiz through Blackboard is it provides statistics on individual test questions, highlighting questions that might be poor discriminators of student performance. Although we had spent considerable time crafting the questions, Blackboard analysis pointed out that not all our questions were of high-quality and we removed one from the results.

Since one goal was to analyze the effectiveness of the tutorial, we wanted to test our students' knowledge both pre- and post-tutorial. Practical considerations regarding administration precluded this option. To attempt to compensate for this, we administered the pre-test, then the tutorial and then the post-test in one sitting where the pre- and post-test questions were the same. This was not ideal and we believe the act of taking the test twice in a short time period may have skewed the results. Optimally, we recommend that either a control group be used instead of the pre- and post-testing in one session or the pre- and post-test questions not be the same.

Recommendations

1. Including experts from outside the Library in the assessment project is particularly helpful in executing the assessment project as well as connecting the Library's work with its campus partners and the University's mission.
2. Basing the assessment method on a recognized tool in higher education gives the assessment project credibility outside the Library.
3. Considering work-loads and technological capabilities, be practical on what can be done. Some assessment is better than no assessment.

Notes

1. Barbara E. Walvoord, Assessment *Clear and Simple* (San Francisco, CA: Jossey-Bass, 2010), 7.
2. Bill Taylor, "Integrity: Academic and Political. A Letter to My Students," accessed September, 2014, http://www.csub.edu/studentconduct/documents/lettertomystudents.pdf
3. International Center for Academic Integrity, "Fundamental Values of Academic Integrity," Fundamental Values Project, accessed May, 2015, http://www.academicintegrity.org/icai/resources-2.php
4. Association of American Colleges & Universities, "VALUE," AACU.org, accessed May, 2015, http://www.aacu.org/value
5. Association of American Colleges & Universities, "Ethical Reasoning VALUE Rubric," AACU.org, accessed May, 2015, https://www.aacu.org/ethical-reasoning-value-rubric
6. Mary J. Allen, *Assessing Academic Programs in Higher Education* (San Francisco, CA: Jossey-Bass, 2004), 138.
7. Phyllis Blumberg, *Assessing and Improving Your Teaching* (San Francisco, CA: Jossey-Bass, 2014), 131.
8. Allen, *Assessing Academic Programs*, 138.

9. Council of Writing Program Administrators, "Defining and Avoiding Plagiarism: The WPA Statement on Best Practices," Writing Program Administrators, accessed May, 2015, http://wpacouncil.org/positions/WPAplagiarism.pdf

10. "The Citation Project: Preventing Plagiarism, Teaching Writing," The Citation Project, accessed May, 2015, http://site.citationproject.net/

11. George Germek, "The Lack of Assessment in the Academic Library Plagiarism Prevention Tutorial," *College & Undergraduate Libraries* 19, no. 1 (2012): 10–11.

12. Germek, "The Lack of Assessment," 15.

1st Year

CHAPTER 3

Cite Me!:
What Sources are Students Using for Research?

Valerie Nye

Institute of American Indian Arts
vnye@iaia.edu

THE INSTITUTE OF AMERICAN Indian Arts (IAIA) is a tribal college in Santa Fe, New Mexico with approximately 400 FTE students. The library is staffed by three professional librarians and one paraprofessional librarian. IAIA has a current and ongoing focus on improving assessment of student learning. All departments, including the library, are required to establish student learning outcomes and to assess them annually.

The library's student learning outcomes at the time of our AiA assessment were numerous, lengthy, and difficult to measure. They included statements such as, "students will examine and compare information from various sources in order to evaluate reliability, validity, accuracy, authority, timeliness, and point of view bias;" and, "students will use various search systems to retrieve information in a variety of formats." Our librarians determined that the most direct way to attempt to assess the library's multiple student learning outcomes was to evaluate the sources students cited in the bibliographies that they created for research projects in their courses. Bibliographies are artifacts of student work that provide evidence of the material students are using as they engage in the research process. We wanted to assess bibliographies to understand the types of material students were using in their research.

The Initial Assessment Project

In the early stages of the assessment project, our librarians planned to work to formally integrate library instruction into all of the first- and second-year general education courses that had a research component. After talking with faculty about course requirements, four general education courses were identified. These courses were offered each semester, each had at least two sections of between ten and twenty students. We planned to provide library instruction to each of these classes and collect the all of the student bibliographies that were submitted as assignments in these classes. We wanted to use students' bibliographies to answer the following questions:

- Are students citing library resources in their bibliographies?
- Are students citing reliable sources in their bibliographies?
- Are students providing enough information in their bibliographies to allow professors and librarians to identify and locate the cited material?

The initial research question for the assessment project was: Do students in general education courses make use of quality information sources?

Based on these questions, our librarians created two rubrics which they used to assess each bibliography. A rubric with scores from 1-4 was created to rate the over-all quality of the references cited in a bibliography. Another rubric with similar scoring was created to rate the over-all accurate use of MLA style for citing sources in a bibliography. We also categorized and counted the number of sources cited in each bibliography using the following categories: library databases, library books, library media, library periodicals, academic websites, non-academic websites, non-library books, and other which included interviews, speeches, and archival material.

After the first semester, it became apparent that our librarians were not going to be able to get consistent participation from all of the faculty teaching all of the general education courses. These initial difficulties included:

- Not being invited to teach library instruction at a time when it would be most beneficial to the students.
- Bibliographies being returned to students immediately after they were graded so our librarians could not access the student work for evaluation.

- Instructors' plans changing throughout the semester causing timing and assignment changes that were not always communicated to the librarians.

Even with successful communication, some faculty members teaching writing and research courses in general education chose not to invite our librarians to provide library instruction and/or chose not to provide us with access to student bibliographies.

Reframing the Assessment Project

Despite these barriers, we were able to effectively and consistently communicate with two faculty members who taught a required general education course, Indigenous Studies 101 (IDST 101). These faculty members had a history of including a library instruction session in their syllabi and they were willing to provide us with access to all of the students' bibliographies throughout the four semester project. Since the faculty members teaching IDST 101 could reliably provide a time for instruction and regularly submitted the bibliographies from the 3-4 research papers students turned in during the semester, the librarians altered the assessment project's focus. A project that was initially an evaluation of all general education research became focused only on IDST 101 instruction and the bibliographies.

The reframed smaller project was a positive change for our librarians. While we continued to market library instruction to faculty teaching all general education courses, narrowing the focus of the assessment project to a specific small set of courses was much more manageable for us. We were able to integrate teaching, communication, and data analysis into our regular workflow. Otherwise attempting to manage an assessment project that included all of the general education courses would have been unmanageable in most semesters.

With a new focus on library instruction for IDST 101, our librarians wanted to use the assessment opportunity to experiment with new teaching methods and use the data that was collected to see how student learning was affected by the way information about the library was delivered to students. The assessment project's question eventually became: Do students engaged in active learning, and with librarians embedded in their classes make use of quality information sources?

We worked with these participating faculty members to set up timely library instruction sessions and regular access to student bibliographies. Our librarians were either provided copies of the bibliographies by the faculty members teaching the class, or were given instructor access the IDST 101 Blackboard course management website where they could download all of the assignments students turned in throughout the semester. Each semester two librarians used the rubrics described earlier to analyze sources and grade the bibliographies. The two librarians met at the end of each semester to discuss and agree upon the category for each source cited. They also negotiated and agreed on a single grade for each bibliography based on the rubrics.

First Semester

In the first semester of assessment, library instruction in IDST 101 was provided in a formal lecture format. The lecture did not require any direct engagement from students. Students watched a librarian demonstrate library databases based on their research topics. Students were also shown an interactive web evaluation tool that they were required by their instructors to work with at a later time. The bibliographies in this first group showed extensive use of non-library sources and non-academic websites.

Second Semester

In the second semester of the assessment project, our librarians began team-teaching the library instruction classes and began experimenting with an active learning technique. In this semester, the librarians spoke to the classes about the differences between the Internet and library databases and then spent a significant amount of time demonstrating how to use several library databases that were relevant to the research students would be conducting for their first assignment. We learned that IDST 101 faculty allowed students to rely heavily on Internet sources, so the class session concluded with students using a worksheet to find information on their topic using the Internet. The students worked in groups to complete the worksheet and reported their findings at the end of the library instruction session. The bibliographies following this initial active learning library instruction session showed an increase in the number of library sources cited. Our librarians, however, were disappointed in the number of non-academic websites that student cited in their bibliographies.

Third Semester

In the third semester of the project our librarians provided an active learning session that had a very strong focus on using the Internet. During the first half of the newly designed library instruction session, students were divided into groups to answer a set of four questions about Google and the reliability of Internet sources. The groups reported their findings to the class, and the librarians engaged in a lengthy discussion about students' reported answers and beliefs. They also provided a very brief demonstration of library databases. The session concluded with an in-class keyword brainstorming exercise that was designed to help students develop a list of key words for their first paper topic.

During this semester, our librarians were embedded in the IDST 101 courses, and attended every course session during the semester. The class also underwent multiple changes independent of the library assessment project that seemed to have a significant impact on student learning and research. Teaching assistants (TAs) were added to the classes and students had a new requirement to meet with TAs at various times between classes. The bibliographies submitted during this semester showed another positive increase in the number of library sources cited and finally a positive increase in the number of academic websites cited.

At the end of this semester, our librarians discussed their experiences attending every class session. The time commitment was enormous, and we thought the impact of attending the classes was only a minor help to students. We recognized, however, that the addition of the TAs to the class was significant and that the TAs often took on a guidance role that the librarians had hoped to establish with students as they engaged with their research topics.

Final Semester

Our librarians decided to abandon the embedded librarian model and focus solely on providing library instruction through a single class session that duplicated the exercise in the third semester of the assessment. The faculty teaching IDST 101 continued to use TAs as active participants in the classroom and research process. The bibliographies submitted in the final semester continued to show a positive increase in the number of reliable Internet sources with a minor decrease in the number of library sources cited.

Conclusion

The data reflect that the changes our librarians made from a lecture format to an active learning environment led to a positive change in the types of material students cited in their bibliographies. An even greater positive change in the type of academic material students cited was seen when students spent a significant time talking with each other and the librarians about reliable Internet sources during the library instruction session. Our interpretation of this data demonstrated that students actively engaging in library instruction with a significant focus and discussion on Internet reliability (and with the support of TAs in their classes) cited more academic sources in their research papers.

Alternative Methods & Additional Ideas

Librarians conducting bibliography analysis at larger institutions might want to consider sampling bibliographies. A sample could occur by taking bibliographies from a single type of class or from a series of classes across the institution. A sample across the institution might alert you to issues that require more focused research.

Some librarians might be interested in negotiating with classroom instructors to assign grades to the bibliographies. Through the assessment project we were able to give time and attention to the bibliographies that the instructors did not always offer. Some options for grading bibliographies include providing a grade that is: purely informational to students and instructors, is incorporated into the student's final paper grade, or is used by the instructor as extra credit for the course.

Libraries engaging in similar projects might also be interested in assessing bibliographies and reading the associated research papers. During one of the semester assessments, we did collect the papers attached to the bibliographies. Overall, we were surprised to find that reading the papers was not an important aspect of evaluating the bibliographies. If an evaluation is being conducted with broad ranging assignments and complex disciplines, however, having access to the text of the research paper could be a critical aspect of understanding the bibliographies.

Analyzing the grades that faculty assign to papers and the grades librarians assign to bibliographies could also be a valuable assessment project. Do highly scored bibliographies correspond to highly scored papers?

Recommendations

For library professionals interested in assessing bibliographies as part of a project similar to ours we have some recommendations based on our experiences:

- Find committed partners. It is important to get a solid commitment from the faculty members with whom you will be working. Analyzing the bibliographies is a time consuming tedious process. If a faculty member stops providing support in the middle of your data collection, a lot of time could be wasted if the project cannot be seen through to completion.
- Extend your timeline. When you are seeking an initial commitment, ask for a longer commitment than you think you will need. If you decide to change something in the middle of the project, or if something changes beyond your control, it is nice to have the extra time built-in to the commitment.
- Don't go it alone. Find librarian colleagues, faculty members, or staff in the institutional research office who can help share the responsibilities of data collection, analysis, and reporting. Having a colleague with whom you can brainstorm teaching techniques and data analysis adds depth to teaching and understanding the assessment results.
- Keep everything. Develop an organized system for maintaining data and retain copies of the bibliographies so that you can gather additional data if it becomes necessary. Partway through our project we sensed that the number of quality sources cited was decreasing from the first assignment to the last assignment. This wasn't something we were initially tracking, but since we had labeled our data by assignment and kept copies of the bibliographies, we were

able to go back and verify that our "senses" about the changing quality of sources was borne out in the data.

- Let the data 'soak.' Over the course of our project we looked at the data in different ways at different times. Over time we asked different questions about the data and had new realizations about how the data could inform our understanding of student learning. Share your data with as many interested people as possible, and encourage them to think about and ask questions about the data.

- Develop a rubric. Test the rubric with samples prior to using the rubric in the formal assessment period. Make sure your rubric is capable of answering all of the questions you have for your assessment project. Changing a rubric in the middle of the project may skew data and impact the consistency of your results.

- Be flexible and aware. Throughout the project, be flexible enough to make changes to the project and your teaching style if it is necessary. Ideally, we would not have changed our teaching style so frequently, but we were learning things about the classes as we looked at the data and we wanted to provide students with the best library experience possible. The changes in teaching required that we collect data for a longer period of time than we originally anticipated, but collecting the data through our alterations let us see that we were making changes in the right direction.

- Does your data show you are moving in a positive direction? Our institution is small, and there was an early concern that we were not seeing "statistically significant" changes in the data we were collecting. Ultimately, our sample of students was too small to create a scientifically accepted "statistically significant" change. Instead of conducting a perfect scientific study, we recognized that any changes we were making in a positive direction were significant for our project. With this in mind our aim was to use the assessment project to make positive changes in student learning.

Further Reading

Gewirtz, Sarah. "Make Your Library Instruction Interactive with Poll Everywhere: An Alternative to Audience Response Systems." *College and Research Libraries News* 73, no. 7 (July 2012): 400–03.

Lambert, Kelly. "Web Evaluation Carousel." *Kelly Lambert Librarian* (blog). May 27, 2015. http://kellylambertlibrarian.weebly.com/instruction.html

Miller, Susan, and Nancy Murillo. "Why Don't Students Ask Librarians for Help? Undergraduate Help Seeking Behavior in Three Academic Libraries." In *College Libraries and Student Culture: What We Now Know*, edited by Andrew D. Asher and Lynda M. Duke, 49–70. Chicago, IL: American Library Association, 2011.

CHAPTER 4

Employing Multiple Methods to Assess Information Literacy in a New Core Curriculum

Kelly Delevan

Le Moyne College
delevakk@lemoyne.edu

MY PARTICIPATION IN ACRL'S Assessment in Action (AiA) project was a catalyst for many different positive outcomes. For me, it sparked an interest in learning more about authentic student learning assessment. Within our library, it inspired the other teaching librarians to join me in planning our first program-level assessment project. At an institutional level, my work on the project ignited a discussion about how best to assess student learning across disciplines, which led to the formation of a college-wide Institutional Assessment Committee. These are all important outcomes, but the project was not without its challenges. In designing and implementing the library assessment project I learned several lessons that continue to shape the way we do assessment at Le Moyne College. For this chapter, I will discuss how necessary openness and flexibility in working with our methods were for us and how they paid off in opportunities to look at student learning from a variety of perspectives.

Embedding the Library in a New Curriculum

In the fall of 2013, Le Moyne College introduced a new core curriculum, requiring First Year students to enroll into a new first year seminar, Core 100. This course introduces students to the ethos of a liberal arts education by guiding them in reflection on their personal engagement with the course material. Students are encouraged to develop a variety of communicative and critical thinking skills and competencies, including written and oral expression and information literacy (IL). Like first- year seminars on many campuses, sections of Core 100 vary in content, and are taught by tenured faculty in a variety of disciplines, though they share learning objectives and a Common Reading. Librarians played a lead role in developing the IL component of the new core by partnering with faculty to deliver IL instruction to all students taking the first year seminar.

A team of five librarians (including myself) worked with the faculty teaching Core 100 to schedule an IL session for each of the 34 sections. Sessions ranged from 50 to 75 minutes, and were centered on a presentation about the "information timeline or information cycle."[1]

Mapping an Assignment and Coordinating Teaching at Scale

After the class, students were given an assignment that required them locate three sources relevant to a pre-determined topic. Since the content of each course varied, the research topics were either tied to the specific section, or as an alternative, were tied to the common reading. Once students located their sources, they were asked to deliver an annotated bibliography that included answers to the questions in Table 4.1. Those questions were then connected to measurable learning outcomes.

Choosing an Appropriate Method

At AiA, I developed the following inquiry question: *How does librarian-led, in-class instruction in Core 100 affect students' selection of sources for the class and do students carry those skills over to a history research project in another class?* I was primarily interested in determining the extent to which students were successful in evaluating sources. I then wondered if the skills

TABLE 4.1. LIBRARY ASSIGNMENT ASSESSMENT MEASURES

ASSIGNMENT PROMPT	LEARNING OUTCOME
What are the citation elements of the source?	Students can cite a source accurately
What method did you use to find the source?	Students describe their search strategy
Is it considered to be scholarly or popular?	Students can identify characteristics of scholarly and popular sources
Is it considered to be a primary, secondary, or tertiary source?	Students can identify characteristics of primary, secondary, and tertiary sources
Why is it (or why is it not) appropriate for your research?	Students can evaluate a source's context and content to determine if it meets their information need

they obtained in Core 100 would transfer as they completed research in History 110: World Civilization (HST 110) in the same semester.

I initially planned to use multiple methods to gather direct and indirect evidence, including a rubric to score the bibliography assignment (direct) and a series of focus groups with students and faculty in Core 100 and HST 110 to gather qualitative evidence (indirect) of student learning. Unfortunately, there was not enough time to schedule focus groups with faculty or students in either course. (Lesson learned: planning for certain kinds of assessment needs to be completed far in advance, depending on the stakeholders involved. Many faculty members are not as available in the summer, and coordinating a project during that time can be difficult.) Since I could not gather indirect evidence of student learning through the focus groups, I decided to amend my inquiry question to focus solely on student success in the Core 100 class: *How does librarian-led, in-class instruction in Core 100 affect students' selection of sources?* I did not have to change my method, but was able to modify my research question appropriately.

With this new question in mind, I continued to focus on the development of a suitable rubric. I like rubrics because they can be used in conjunction with grading, they offer a clear set of expectations for student success, and rubric rows can be mapped to learning outcomes. Many learning management systems allow rubrics to be attached to an assignment, which when graded online allows for the simultaneous collection of assessment data. Designing a good rubric can be challenging, but there is an abundance of rubrics available to use as models. I adapted one of Purdue's annotated bibliography rubrics for this assignment.[2]

While my rubric was primarily developed to perform course-level assessment, I was also interested in using these data begin to measure whether the library was achieving its goals of teaching IL concepts at the program level (i.e. the Core Curriculum). That required us to map the assessment to the library's program learning goals. Our goals for 2013 were aligned with the 2001 ACRL Standards for Information Literacy[3] (see Table 4.2 below).

TABLE 4.2. LIBRARY ASSIGNMENT RUBRIC

ASSIGNMENT PROMPT	LEARNING OUTCOME	ACRL STANDARD/ PERFORMANCE INDICATOR
What are the citation elements of the source?	Students can cite a source accurately	ACRL 2.5
What method did you use to find the source?	Students describe their search strategy	ACRL 1.4, 2.3
Is it considered to be scholarly or popular?	Students can identify characteristics of scholarly and popular sources	ACRL 1.2
Is it considered to be a primary, secondary, or tertiary source?	Students can identify characteristics of primary, secondary, and tertiary sources	ACRL 1.2
Why is it (or why is it not) appropriate for your research?	Students can evaluate a source's context and content to determine if it meets their information need	ACRL 3.1, 3.2

Using Canvas to Score Rubrics

At the time of my project, Le Moyne had just begun using a new learning management system (LMS), Canvas. The outcomes reporting features of that system offered a chance to use the rubric for both grading and assessment. Our librarians graded the assignment using the rubric and the total score was sent to the student and the course instructor. The rubric was also aligned with outcomes that mapped directly to the ACRL standards. Canvas' rubrics allow for designating a "mastery threshold" that can be preset prior to data collection. Since this was a first year course, we decided that students who received a score equivalent to "meeting expectations" or "exceeding expectations" would achieve mastery. The best part about using Canvas was that the outcomes were created at a level above each individual course, which allowed for outcomes reporting across all 34 sections of Core 100. This library assignment became the first learning assessment project that actually reported data on student success within the core program.

Limitations with Rubrics

Norming and Reliability

Norming is the process that allows everyone using the rubric to ensure its criteria are interpreted consistently.[4] I learned about norming during my AiA work, but I wish I had been more aware of the process when I was designing my rubric. We did not norm the rubric before the class sessions occurred. Because of this, our inter-rater reliability (i.e., the degree of agreement among all raters) was not has high as we would have liked.

Rubric Design

The rubric itself (see Figure 4.1) proved problematic. While we were very detailed in explaining the criteria for the highest and lowest levels of proficiency, we were not specific enough in the intermediate level which made it hard to score. We set up the rubric to score a possible 100 points so that it could easily be used for grading, but it forced us to scale the rubric rows unevenly. This presented a problem when it came time to visualize our data. Also, in trying to meet a total of 100 points, we added rubric rows for research topic and grammar that were not part of our assessment design.

FIGURE 4.1. ANNOTATED BIBLIOGRAPHY RUBRIC

CRITERIA	RATINGS			TOTAL POINTS	ACRL STANDARD
	Exceeds Expectations	**Meets Expectations**	**Does Not Meet Expectations**		
Research Topic	n/a	The research topic is clearly written at top of the worksheet. **5 pts**	The research topic is not stated at the top of the worksheet. **0 pts**	**5**	
Source— Citation	All necessary citation elements are presented. **5 pts**	Some necessary citation elements are missing, or extraneous elements are present. **3 pts**	There is no citation. **0 pts**	**5**	2.5c, 2.5d
Source— Research Process	Student thoroughly explains research process (search engine, catalog, database used, keywords entered, etc.) **5 pts**	Student only briefly explains the research process. **3 pts**	Student does not explain the research process. **0 pts**	**5**	1.4b, 2.3a-c
Source— Evaluation— Authority	Student thoroughly distinguishes what makes the source scholarly/popular. Discussion of audience, format, producer included in explanation. **5 pts**	Student thoroughly distinguishes what makes the source scholarly/popular, but does not correctly explain the characteristics (audience, format, producer, etc.). **3 pts**	Student incorrectly distinguishes sources as scholarly or popular. **0 pts**	**5**	1.2a, 1.2d

FIGURE 4.1. ANNOTATED BIBLIOGRAPHY RUBRIC

CRITERIA	RATINGS			TOTAL POINTS	ACRL STANDARD
	Exceeds Expectations	**Meets Expectations**	**Does Not Meet Expectations**		
Source—Evaluation—Source Type	Student thoroughly distinguishes what makes the source primary, secondary or tertiary. Discussion of characteristics of source (time created, author, point of view, etc.) is included in explanation. **5 pts**	Student thoroughly distinguishes what makes the source primary, secondary or tertiary, but does not correctly explain the characteristics of source (time created, author, point of view, etc.). **3 pts**	Student incorrectly distinguishes sources as primary, secondary, or tertiary. **0 pts**	5	1.2a, 1.2e
Source—Context	Student thoroughly explains why the source is or is not appropriate for the research topic (discussion of contents of source, important features or statistics that might be used, discussion of author, discussion of reviews, etc.). **10 pts**	Student only briefly explains why the source is or is not appropriate for the research topic. There is little discussion of course contents. **5 pts**	Student does not explain why the source is or is not appropriate for the research topic. **0 pts**	10	3.1, 3.2
Writing	Well written; contains less than 3 grammatical/spelling errors. **5 pts**	Well written; contains 3-5 grammatical/spelling errors. **3 pts**	Poorly written; and/or contains more than 5 grammatical/spelling errors. **0 pts**	5	

Data Collection and Analysis

We were the first department on our campus to use Canvas' outcomes reporting features and spent several weeks learning the system as well as deciding how best to structure the outcomes so that they could be used for program-level assessment. Once outcomes were embedded at the program level and the assignments were scored, we were able to export a large set of raw data. I relied heavily on our Institutional Research office for help extrapolating and interpreting the data.

Exploring Alternate Methods

The rubric, while flawed, still allowed me to assess the extent to which students mastered the learning outcomes. This was really useful at the program level, because I was able to report our work to members of the Core Curriculum Committee tasked with assessing student learning. Our project showed that 85% of first year students mastered (at an introductory level) a set of IL skills as measured by a library assignment.

In hindsight, I realize that other methods might have been used to evaluate student learning in this environment. Early on in the AiA project, I was interested in measuring how students transferred skills they learned in one class to another class. I was disappointed that I was unable to complete that part of my project. I really wanted to try assessing student learning with a more reflective method, like focus groups or interviews. However in working through the rubric scoring for the annotated bibliography I realized that I could possibly apply a different method to analyze the assignments themselves. The annotated bibliographies that students created in Core 100 included a reflective element, in that we asked students to *describe* the method they used to find their sources. I saw an opportunity to look at whether the research tool played a role in students' ability to evaluate the sources that they found. By doing so I could also observe possible themes in the way students searched for information. I had never participated in any qualitative assessment projects before this time but I was inspired by my experiences in the AiA cohort to dive in and try something new. In library and information science research, the method of content analysis has been praised for its flexibility.[5] It allows researchers to analyze and make inferences about the context of textual information. I had textual information in the form of the students' descriptions of their research processes which represented a fairly rich dataset. I must stress that this was an informal analysis—I was simply experimenting with aspects of the method. I generated a random sample (n=60) of scored papers and performed an informal content analysis of the students' answers to the question "What method did you use to find your source?"

I read their answers to identify the various research tools that were used. Next, I coded them for the research tool and the type of source they located. For example, when a student mentioned JSTOR, that got coded as a "database" and when a student mentioned the find books page, it got coded as "catalog", and so on. Table 4.3 below provides a snippet view of how I coded the answers.

TABLE 4.3. CODING EXAMPLE OF STUDENTS' RESEARCH TOOLS

Research Process—Text Copy	
Library website, catalog, find books, books = Catalog	
Database, (name of database), find articles, articles = Database	**Research Tool**
Google, search engine, search online, websites = Google	
Google scholar = Google Scholar	
Asked a librarian = librarian help	
I searched the **library website for books** using the keywords "disenfranchised grief."	Catalog
First I went on the library website and clicked on the **Find Articles** tab. Then I searched the EBSCO Host **database** for wiki leaks and refined the search by choosing Scholarly (peer reviewed) **Journals**. Then I looked through the sources and found articles with titles relevant to the topic.	Database
First I went to the History Research Guide on the Le Moyne library website. From there I chose the **America: History and Life database**. Next, I typed in the keywords "bartleby the scrivener". I picked this article because the pertaining abstract seemed relevant to my question. My next step was to follow the link to the article to **www.jstor. org**. I was then able to open a PDF of article I was looking for. My strategy was to first find the topic that I needed to research, which was American History, and from there I weeded through the articles to find which one seemed most relevant.	Database

TABLE 4.3. CODING EXAMPLE OF STUDENTS' RESEARCH TOOLS

I went to the library webpage and clicked the tab **"Find Books"** and then I searched Haudenosaunee. I looked through the book choices seeing which ones were about the Haudenosaunee Indians' lifestyle and important events of their lives. This is how I found my sources for my research.	Catalog
I found this source by searching on the **library's database**. I entered "clothing" into the keyword and stumbled across this **book**. I then wrote down the numbers corresponding with this **book** and went to the library to find it off of the shelves.	Catalog
I found this source on the Le Moyne Library online site in the research guides section. I went to the history section and then I went to the **databases** and chose **JSTOR** and typed in my research topic.	Database
How I found this webpage was I did a **Google** search of "Workday of a Medical Doctor". When I did this looked at the name of the **websites** first to look for any well-known websites. After I found the U.S. News and World Report, the site and information looked to be a creditable source.	Google
I went to **Google Scholar** and searched "Bartleby the Scrivener criticisms" and came up with this book about the critics of Bartleby.	Google Scholar

After I gathered data on the research tool that students were using to locate their sources, I learned that students used database to find sources the most, followed by the library catalog, and Google (see Figure 4.2).

FIGURE 4.2. STUDENT USE OF RESEARCH TOOLS

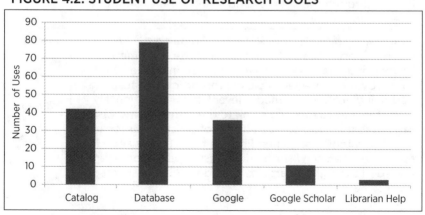

While this was just a practice exercise, I was excited to learn more about how students tackled the library assignment. I was pleased to see that students used library resources at a high rate. I hope to have the opportunity to explore the use of content analysis in a more formal research setting.

Conclusion

I would encourage librarians who are new to assessment to be willing to experiment with methods with which they are unfamiliar. Even if you do not obtain reportable results, informal results can still provide you with valuable insight into the student learning experience and can help you determine future research directions. Assessment should inform change—sometimes a change in method can provide you with a new and interesting perspective. My participation in AiA coincided with our participation in a new core curriculum, and it generated positive momentum among our teaching librarians. We are heading into our third year of teaching in Core 100 with a new lesson plan that maps to elements of the new Information Literacy framework. I look forward to improving upon our assessment design, and experimenting with new methods along the way.

Notes

1. I find the concept of the information cycle (or timeline) to be an effective teaching tool and adapted my lesson from several different libraries including Virginia Tech (http://www.lib.vt.edu/help/research/information-time-line.html). For a critical approach to teaching the information cycle see Maria T. Accardi, Emily Drabinski and Alana Kumbier, eds, *Critical Library Instruction: Theories and Methods*, (Duluth, Minn.: Library Juice Press, 2010), 47.
2. Sean Mitsein, "English 106: First-Year Composition, Annotated Bibliography Rubric," January 12, 2014, Purdue University, accessed May 15, 2015, http://web.ics.purdue.edu/~smitsein/English_106/Assessments/Annotated_Bibliography_Assessment.html
3. Association of College and Research Libraries, "Information Literacy Competency Standards of Higher Education," 2001, accessed May 15, 2015, http://www.ala.org/acrl/standards/informationliteracycompetency

4. For information on the norming process see Claire Holmes and Megan Oak-leaf, "The Official (and Unofficial) Rules for Norming Rubrics Successfully," *Journal of Academic Librarianship*, 39:6 (2013): 599–602.

5. Marilyn Domas White and Emily Marsh, "Content Analysis: A Flexible Methodology," *Library Trends*, 55:1 (2006): 22–45

CHAPTER 5

Assessing Student Learning and Faculty-Librarian Collaboration with a Mixed-Methods Approach

Veronica Arellano Douglas

St. Mary's College of Maryland
viarellano@smcm.edu

IDEALLY, ASSESSMENT SHOULD BE an integral component of our teaching, one that informs how our students learn and highlights what we as professors, librarians, and administrators can do to help facilitate meaningful classroom experiences.[1] Yet because the push for student learning assessment in higher education has only recently hit a critical point,[2] many of us have inherited curricula originally developed without integrated assessment. Retrofitting student learning assessment into these programs can be a challenge. In addition to creating authentic assessment practices, there's the crucial task of convincing administrators, faculty, and librarians that this new work is important. Some higher education accrediting bodies have made that argument for us,[3] but it can still be a painstaking effort to apply assessment practices to curricula—and all its disparate, moving parts—created without assessment in mind.

The St. Mary's College of Maryland Assessment in Action (AiA) project was, without question, a retrofitting of assessment into an existing educational program. In 2008 the college adopted a new core curriculum centered on the four liberal arts skills of written expression, oral expression, critical thinking and information literacy.[4] Our librarians developed information literacy (IL) learning outcomes and a liaison librarian program for the cornerstone of this new curriculum, the First Year Seminar (FYS), but did not integrate assessment activities into this critical course. Each year the frequency of library-led classes for each FYS section was recorded along with different aspects of FYS faculty-librarian interaction. The College had also declined to develop a comprehensive assessment program for this newly adopted curriculum. In the first year of its implementation, FYS students gathered their coursework into e-portfolios that faculty and administrators were unsure how to effectively assess. Much of this uncertainty stemmed from the FYS's lack of common class topics, syllabi, and assignments, a result of instructor's freedom to develop unique subject-based seminars. The e-portfolio was abandoned after the first year, replaced with surveys that asked students to rate their perceived level of competency in each of the liberal arts skills at the start and end of the seminar.

A Focus on Collaboration

With our AiA project, we wanted to move beyond counting classes and affective surveys towards more meaningful student learning assessment. Of particular concern to librarians was the relationship between students' IL abilities and the level of faculty-librarian collaboration in each FYS section. Librarian involvement in the FYS has always been at the discretion of the instructor. Despite continuous outreach efforts, FYS instructors' receptiveness to collaboration with librarians varied significantly. This caused our librarians to question whether the uneven nature of their collaborative relationships with FYS faculty had an impact on students' development of IL skills.

To answer this question, we required a diverse group of individuals with different perspectives on the FYS. The Writing Center Director, Library Director, Dean of the Core Curriculum, librarians, and FYS faculty comprised a team that examined student learning in relation to FYS faculty-librarian collaboration *as it existed at the time of the Assessment in Action project.* Our methods fell squarely in the camp of "action research," with an emphasis on how our assessment results could be used to improve student learning.[5]

Prioritizing Outcomes

Our team was fortunate to have a working definition of information literacy in the form of our FYS learning outcomes. Yet the extensive, detailed nature of our outcomes made it difficult to assess them all within this one project.[6] We instead opted to assess the outcomes we felt were most important for our students to meet. These included familiarity with the library's facilities, collections, and librarians; an ability to construct a research question or thesis; and incorporation of appropriate, relevant information sources into research assignments.

A Mixed-Methods Approach

To explore the relationship between students' information literacy abilities and faculty-librarian collaboration, our team adopted a mixed-methods approach. It included five components: 1) a start-of-semester survey on students' familiarity with libraries, librarians, and library resources; 2) an end-of-semester survey on students' self-reported use of library resources and contact with librarians; 3) a rubric-based assessment of student research essays; 4) a survey of librarians on their collaboration with FYS faculty; and 5) a survey of FYS faculty on their collaboration with librarians and integration of IL into their seminar (this was later replaced with faculty interviews).

This summary paints a rather neat picture of our project, but as anyone who has coordinated a large-scale assessment program can attest, the decisions to use particular methods and the mode in which they are carried out are often more complex than initially expected. By elaborating on our team's choices, resultant failures and successes, and suggestions for alternative methods, my hope is that other project coordinators can make more informed decisions for future assessment efforts.

What Do Our Students Already Know?

The librarians on our team were intrigued by the 2013 Project Information Literacy (PIL) report *Learning the Ropes: How Freshman Conduct Course Research Once They Enter College*.[7] It provided an interesting model for answering a question we asked each fall: What do our first year students know about libraries and research? Using the PIL study as a guide, we created a short survey to distribute to all FYS students and planned to conduct follow-up interviews with a small group of volunteers from our respondent pool. The librarians on the team developed the survey instrument, which was reviewed by the Dean of the Core Curriculum, a psychologist well versed in survey design. The Dean recommended distributing paper surveys during the first week of classes, which was done by each seminar's peer mentor at the Dean's request. Although it created more work in terms of collection and data entry, this paper-and-pencil method was the best way to ensure a high response rate.

Our initial intention to supplement our survey with a series of student interviews fell through after the reality of a busy fall semester set in. This was a loss for our project. It would have given students the opportunity to speak freely about their library and research-related concerns and share the reasoning behind their survey responses.[8]

In addition, our project would have benefited from the establishment of some kind of early semester benchmark of students' research abilities. This is a tricky thing to pull off well. No professor is inclined to assign a research paper during the first few weeks of classes, much less one teaching first year students. Yet perhaps with additional planning we could have worked with FYS faculty to create a benchmarking assignment early in the semester or implement a short IL pre-test, which has been shown to be useful when determining students' entry-level knowledge.[9]

Assessing Students' Information Literacy Abilities

The bulk of our assessment project focused on two activities at the end of the fall semester: a second student survey and a rubric-based assessment of research essays. Like its start-of-semester counterpart, the second survey was distributed in paper format to all FYS students. It was designed to gather data on how often students were visiting the library, what library resources they used, and whether they consulted librarians for research assistance. The main limitation of the survey was its reliance on self-reported data as opposed to measuring actual student activity. Yet the alternatives—gathering students' library circulation data, logging their interactions with librarians, monitoring their research activity—seemed both unrealistic and a gross violation of privacy. Although by no means painting a complete picture, the information we gleaned from this survey was a useful snapshot. Again, as with the earlier survey, our story could have been enriched by interviews with students.

One hitch in administering this second survey concerned our timing. Because we distributed this instrument at the end of the semester, perhaps too near the end of classes and finals week, we had a much lower response rate than for the initial survey (62% as opposed to 98%). Our survey distributors and collectors, the peer mentors, were less reliable at the end of the fall semester when schoolwork and other responsibilities are more demanding. It's important to consider the ebb and flow of work during any semester when planning assessment activities.

Rubric Evaluation of Student Essays

Our team had a strong desire to supplement survey data with an evaluation of student work. As previously mentioned, there is no common curriculum within the FYS program. Given this reality, our team used the syllabi from each FYS section to identify classes with research assignments that possessed elements reflected in the IL learning outcomes we'd chosen to assess. The faculty of these sections were contacted and asked to share student submissions for assessment. Many faculty would only do so with student approval, which was respected. Ultimately, our team collected 103 student essays from nine different FYS sections. We then used the assignment requirements for each essay to develop a rubric.

It was a challenging endeavor. We did not want to alter the curriculum of the FYS and made a conscious effort to assess student work within the confines of the existing program structure. Therefore we retroactively developed a rubric to assess student work within the context of current educational realities. Developing this rubric was a concerted effort between the librarians, Library Director, and Writing Center Director (also an FYS instructor). After our first rubric creation meeting two facts became clear: 1) the way librarians and FYS instructors think about research essays is quite different, and 2) none of us had ever created a rubric before, and it showed. Despite finding multiple examples of IL rubrics online—from the AAC&U Value rubric to those in the RAILS project[10]—we struggled to agree on a structure and criteria. We needed help, and we needed to look outside our assessment team to get it. One of our educational studies professors teaches rubric creation to future teachers and generously offered her time and expertise to our team. Her suggestions for an effective rubric structure and criteria, as well as her guidance on the rubric norming process were invaluable. This professor's involvement made us painfully aware that we should have included a member of the educational studies department on our team at our project's inception.

Characterizing Collaboration

Assessing student learning was just one component of our project plan. We also wanted to relate student IL abilities to the degree of collaboration between FYS faculty and their liaison librarian. At the end of the fall semester, all FYS liaison librarians completed a survey on their interactions with FYS faculty, their influence on section syllabi and assignments, and their time spent teaching students in that section. To accomplish this, a subset of our project team developed an operational definition of collaboration for the purposes of this project, then created an instrument that could be used to evaluate the data gleaned from our librarian survey. Each librarian-faculty pair was scored on a 5-point collaboration scale where the highest level of collaboration was defined as working together to create IL assignments and lesson plans.

Gathering Faculty Perspectives

Before scoring each librarian-faculty pair according to this collaboration scale, the team wanted to gather FYS faculty input on their interactions with librarians. We were also interested in faculty's overall experiences incorporating IL concepts into their seminars. Unfortunately, our tactic of reaching faculty through a print survey didn't work. The response rate was abysmal; we received only a handful of partially completed surveys. Thus the librarian survey data became our measure of faculty-librarian collaboration within the FYS.

Despite this setback, we were still eager to hear from faculty about their experience incorporating IL into the FYS. The team decided to gather this data in person, with a few targeted interviews with FYS faculty from different disciplines. There was some concern by the College's IRB about the comfort level of faculty when discussing their teaching relationships with their librarian colleagues. So we took great care to ensure that the interviewer was not the liaison librarian to any of the faculty interviewed. All interview recordings and transcripts were kept confidential and only viewed by the interviewer and the team leader. The team leader coded the transcripts and summarized findings for the rest of the team, thus maintaining faculty confidentiality.

These interviews offered little insight into the faculty-librarian teaching relationship other than brief, polite comments, which was likely a result of faculty being interviewed by a librarian. This method did, however, succeed in giving a voice to faculty who often felt as though they were struggling to meet the instructional requirements of the FYS. The combination of teaching content, the four liberal arts skills, and "college success" behaviors was intimidating. These interviews helped place faculty's pedagogical decisions into context, and helped us understand that information literacy was just one piece of a continuously shifting instructional puzzle.

Alternative Methods and Parting Thoughts

In reflecting on our assessment methods, the argument could be made that we relied too heavily on survey data, a habit common among LIS researchers.[11] Our experience with faculty interviews was so insightful that any future assessment efforts will likely include interviews or focus groups to help contextualize results. The recent boom of ethnographic research in libraries has shown that these participatory methods can highlight issues beyond those previously identified by researchers.[12] This is not to say that surveys are ineffective or that we regret using them in this project. Much of the comprehensive data on students' interactions with library resources could not have been ethically sourced without a survey. An assessment team would simply benefit from the perspective offered by additional qualitative methods.

A rubric-based evaluation of student essays proved to be a successful means of authentic student learning assessment, one that we would likely replicate in future years and in other educational contexts. It is easy to imagine the application of rubric-based assessment to other types of cumulative assignments in the FYS, such as final research presentations and posters. The rubric would need to be modified to suit the medium, but the core of its evaluative characteristics of IL would remain the same.

Although we were pleased with the information gathered from our pre-assessment activity, having some benchmark of students' research abilities would have been helpful. This is important to consider when charting not just performance but development of students' abilities over time. Some alternatives to a start-of-semester research project, which would likely earn the ire of both students and faculty, might be in-class or homework assignments that focus on students acquiring and evaluating information sources. This of course requires a depth of faculty-librarian collaboration that may not be present in an educational program, so it is important to choose a method that makes sense for your particular educational context.

Lastly, I cannot stress enough how important it is to have a diverse assessment team. As crucial as librarians are to students' IL education, we don't teach in a vacuum. Faculty must be incorporated into authentic student learning assessment. Their expertise was critical to the development and completion of our assessment project and had the unintended but pleasant side effect of highlighting the involvement of librarians in undergraduate education. Our work on this project changed the perception of librarians, to some degree, from skill-based instructors to potential teaching partners, which is a solid foundation upon which to build future collaborative relationships for meaningful education and assessment.

Notes

1. Debra L. Gilchrist, "A Twenty Year Path: Learning about Assessment; Learning from Assessment," *Communications in Information Literacy* 3, no. 2 (2010): 70–79, doi:10.7548/cil.v3i2.104.
2. Peter Hernon and Robert E. Dugan, *Outcomes Assessment in Higher Education: Views and Perspectives* (Westport, Conn.: Libraries Unlimited, 2004).
3. Meredith Gorran Farkas, Lisa Janicke Hinchliffe and Amy Harris Houk, "Bridges and Barriers: Factors Influencing a Culture of Assessment in Academic Libraries," *College & Research Libraries* 76, no. 2 (March 2015): 150–69, doi:10.5860/crl.76.2.150.
4. For a complete description of the St. Mary's College of Maryland's Core Curriculum, see http://www.smcm.edu/academics/corecurriculum/
5. Andy Townsend, *Action Research: The Challenges of Understanding and Researching Practice* (Maidenhead: McGraw-Hill Education, 2013).
6. For the original St. Mary's College of Maryland FYS Information Literacy Competency Standards, see: https://smcmaiaproject.wordpress.com/fys-learning-outcomes/original-fys-il-competency-standards-2007/
7. Allison Head, *Learning the Ropes: How Freshmen Conduct Course Research Once They Enter College* (Seattle, WA: Project Information Literacy, 2013).

8. Rebecca Halpern, Christopher Eaker, John Jackson and Daina Bouquin, "#DitchTheSurvey: Expanding Methodological Diversity in LIS Research," *In the Library with the Lead Pipe* (blog), March 11, 2015, http://www.intheli-brarywiththeleadpipe.org/2015/ditchthesurvey-expanding-methodologi-cal-diversity-in-lis-research/

9. Elise Boyas, Lois D. Bryan and Tanya Lee, "Conditions Affecting the Useful-ness of Pre- and Post-Tests for Assessment Purposes," *Assessment & Evalua-tion in Higher Education* 37, no. 4 (January 1, 2012): 427–37.

10. "Information Literacy Value Rubric," Association of American Colleges & Universities, https://www.aacu.org/value/rubrics/information-literacy (accessed January, 2014); "Rubric Assessment of Information Literacy Skills (RAILS)," Institute of Museum and Library Services, http://railsontrack.info (accessed January, 2014).

11. Halpern, "#DitchTheSurvey"

12. Lynda M. Duke and Andrew D. Asher, *College Libraries and Student Culture: What We Now Know* (Chicago: American Library Association, 2012); Nancy Fried Foster and Susan Gibbons, *Studying Students: The Undergraduate Re-search Project at the University of Rochester* (Chicago: Association of College and Research Libraries, 2007); Nancy Fried Foster, *Studying Students : A Second Look* (Chicago: Association of College and Research Libraries, 2013); Patricia Ann Steele, David Cronrath, Sandra Parsons Vicchio and Nancy Fried Foster, *The Living Library: An Intellectual Ecosystem* (Chicago: Associa-tion of College and Research Libraries, 2014).

CHAPTER 6

Assessment of Library Instruction within General Education Learning Outcomes and Academic Support Programs:

Determining Impact on Student Research Skills, Confidence, and Retention

Diane Prorak

University of Idaho Library
prorak@uidaho.edu

AT THE UNIVERSITY OF Idaho our ACRL Assessment in Action Project (AiA) had two parts. We assessed library instruction for first-year students, both in *general education* and *academic support courses*. Different methods were used for each of the groups due to the nature of the courses and characteristics of the student groups. Our results showed academic growth in both sets of students, and our process led to growth in our own understanding of library instruction assessment.

Part 1: General Education Assessment

This assessment focused on student learning in Integrated Seminar (ISEM) courses. ISEM101 courses are thematic, first-year experience courses required of all new freshmen at the University of Idaho. Each section focuses on a different topic but incorporates similar learning outcomes (such as research skills) throughout the semester. Librarians frequently teach information literacy sessions in connection with research assignments as part of the courses. These courses had been significantly revised in 2011 as part of many changes to the University of Idaho general education program.

Methods

The project began by collaborating with the Director of the General Education (DGE) program, who was also initiating a process to assess its recently revised program. The assessment process began with the DGE soliciting faculty to participate. They agreed to have their section of ISEM101 students participate in the assessment program and submit essays (with bibliographies) for the process. Students in the five sample ISEM101 sections wrote essays at the beginning and end of the semester. Each section received library instruction after the first essay, including a face-to-face session and a tailored online research guide related to course topics for the second essay. Each essay included a bibliography. Our library had assessed bibliographies in the past, but without the context the essays provided. We generally only looked at bibliographies separate from the essays and usually only after the final research paper. Thus we could determine if the bibliographies met academic expectations but not if students learned anything about research during the semester. With this project, not only were we able to see bibliographies both before and after library instruction, but we were part of a larger assessment project which provided more legitimacy and university buy-in.

The methods were determined working with the DGE. He recruited the sections and wrote both essay requirements for the sample sections while I added requirements for the bibliography. We met with instructors during the summer before the kickoff semester to discuss the standard essay requirements and lesson plans. The first essay related to the Common Read book for that year (which encourages the University and wider community all to read the same book) but the second essay could fit the theme of the particular ISEM101 course. About a year before this project began, a university task force had developed rubrics for assessing learning outcomes based on the AACU Value Rubric.[1] We decided to use the university's rubric for the essays, while adapting the library's standard rubric for bibliographies.

A faculty team was recruited by the DGE to assess the essays. When the faculty assessment group met for a norming session, concerns were raised about some parts of the general rubric which did not seem to apply to the current assessment task. The group suggested changes to the rubric and recommended the development of a scoring sheet to facilitate more consistency, which were implemented. The revised rubric was used to assess the first essays, which measured students' writing skills as they entered college. Faculty completed the process on their own and submitted scores to the DGE.

After one semester of this assessment process, the results showed student improvement in both essay and bibliography quality. The essay ratings increased from 1.16 to 1.55 (4-point scale) and the bibliography ratings increased from 1.73 to 2.5 (3-point scale). These scores demonstrated growth in the writing and research skills of these students.

While the assessment process had provided insights into student learning, there had been fewer essays submitted at the end of the semester (N=42) than at the beginning (N=95) and faculty felt the workload of two essays (in addition to other coursework) had been too heavy for students. We consulted with the University's Office of Institutional Research to compare retention numbers for the library-instructed sections to sections without library instruction, but the results were inconclusive. It may be the sample size was too small to see changes in retention. Other studies have shown associations between retention and library use in the first semester[2], first-year seminars[3], and collaboration of librarians in first-year experience courses[4], all of which were part of our methods.

Thus we began looking at changes, which are in the process of being fully implemented. Instead of assessing the same students in one course, student essays will be assessed once in ISEM101 (to get a first-year baseline), then again in the upper division general education course ISEM301. Essay ratings from the first year will be compared to the student cohort at an upper level. With a longer time frame, we can better see student learning and growth but keep the workload for both students and faculty more manageable. This should also increase the sample size since the workload will be distributed across time as well as population.

Discussion

One of the primary benefits of this research project was the collaboration on assessment with the DGE, which will lead to continued and improved assessment for upcoming years. As a result of this project, faculty from across campus became involved in assessing general education and information literacy, as well as developing effective methods to assess the success of student learning. By developing effective assessment, we can progress toward answering the critical question of what role the library plays in the important measurement of student success and retention, and help our universities improve in those areas.

Part 2: Academic Support Programs

Another part of our project involved collaboration with first-year courses in the Academic Support and Access Programs. These eight-week, INTR101 courses are titled "Focus on Success" and assist students in developing academic skills and strategies useful in their other courses. Many of these students are first generation, special needs or at-risk.

Methods

For the INTR101 classes we measured student confidence in using the library for research and also student perceptions of the library. Students in ten sections filled out surveys about library use, research confidence and library perceptions before a library session that provided a walk-around "self-guided tour" in small groups. It was a scavenger hunt activity designed to help these students become more familiar with the library's resources in an active way. Some activity questions were adjusted to fit the theme of their class section (e.g. Hispanic history), but there was less focus on academics and more on helping the students feel comfortable with the library. In Idaho, many students come from very small towns with very small libraries, and have never navigated a library as large as ours, so it can seem intimidating. After the session, students filled out another survey to record their confidence and impressions.

Students rated confidence on a 5-point scale. Library confidence increased 80% after library instruction. Comments were analyzed and the results grouped by theme as well as positive/negative feelings. Before instruction, many students commented on the large size and different organization compared to libraries they had used before. Students were also asked after the session what they would recommend to a friend who needed to do research. The library and its staff were highly recommended as resources.

Discussion

We asked the Office of Institutional Research to compare first-to-second-year retention for these sections and sections in previous years without the library sessions, but no difference was found. Once again, a large part of the benefit of this project was the partnerships it created with the Academic Support team. Students and instructors were very positive about the activities, so the library activity has become a standard part of the courses. The library is also viewed as a part of the student support network in the University. In addition, our project demonstrated the library's interest in contributing to the academic success of students, in documenting the impact of our work on them, and working towards continuous improvement of our programs.

Project Discussion

The assessment methods in this project were practical and sustainable. We looked for ways to either collaborate or use methods that could be quickly and easily done. The collaboration with General Education has proved to be very beneficial. Our partnership gave legitimacy to the library's information literacy program as a part of General Education and showed our dedication to assessment and continuous improvement. Now information literacy will be a part of the General Education assessment. The faculty on the recently codified "General Education Assessment Committee" will also be helping assess our program—making it sustainable. In addition, collaboration with Academic Support has led to further visibility within student support services.

Though we have not been able to show that library instruction impacted retention, we continue to work on methods to achieve that goal.

At our recent University accreditation visit, the library's assessment work and involvement in this project caught the positive attention of one of the members of the team. Overall the University Administration has been very satisfied with our assessment methods and results. The AiA assessment project was very successful in bringing our library instruction program assessment into the larger university community and bringing positive attention to and new partnerships for our library instruction program.

Notes

1. Association of American Colleges and Universities (AACU), "VALUE Rubric Development Project," AACU, accessed May 26, 2015, http://www.aacu. org/value/rubrics
2. Krista M. Soria, Jan Fransen and Shane Nackerud, "Stacks, Serials, Search Engines, and Students' Success: First-Year Undergraduate Students' Library Use, Academic Achievement, and Retention," *Journal of Academic Librarianship* 40, no. 1 (2014): 84–91.
3. ACT, Inc. "What Works In Student Retention?" *Fourth National Survey. Public Four-Year Colleges and Universities Report. ACT, Inc.* (2010).
4. Jesus E. Sanabria, "The Library as an Academic Partner in Student Retention and Graduation: The Library's Collaboration with the Freshman Year Seminar Initiative at the Bronx Community College," *Collaborative Librarianship* 5, no. 2 (2013): 94–100.
5. For more detail about the rubrics used and the findings, please see our AiA project LibGuide: http://libguides.uidaho.edu/AiAIdaho

Further Reading

Belanger, Jackie, Rebecca Bliquez and Sharleen Mondal. "Developing a Collaborative Faculty-Librarian Information Literacy Assessment Project." *Library Review*, 61, no. 2 (2012): 68–91.

Bluemle, Stephanie R., Amanda Y. Makula and Margaret W. Rogal. "Learning by Doing: Performance Assessment of Information Literacy across the First-Year Curriculum," *College & Undergraduate Libraries*, 20, no. 3/4 (September 2013): 298–313.

Palsson, Felicia and Carrie L. McDade. "Factors Affecting the Successful Implementation of a Common Assignment for First-Year Composition Information Literacy." *College & Undergraduate Libraries* 21, no. 2 (May 2014): 193–209.

CHAPTER 7

Impact of Information Literacy Instruction on the Success of First Year Composition Students

Maryellen Allen

Tampa Library, University of South Florida
mallen@usf.edu

THE UNIVERSITY OF SOUTH Florida (USF) is a large, urban, research institution located in west-central Florida. With an enrollment of over 48,000 students USF stands as one of the top-rated doctoral granting institutions in the state. The University is a system that includes three separately accredited institutions by the Southern Association of Colleges and Schools. These include USF Tampa, USF St. Petersburg, and USF Sarasota-Manatee. USF Tampa, the main campus, houses over a dozen colleges as well as USF Health.

About the USF Libraries

USF Libraries support the research and reference needs of one of Florida's premier research universities with extensive print and electronic holdings, and a wide variety of student and faculty services. The University of South Florida Library System is comprised of three campus libraries and two special libraries—the Health Science Library and the Louis de la Parte Mental

Health Institute Library. USF's main research library and Special Collections department are centrally located on the Tampa Campus and serve as one of the campus' busiest student-centered study and meeting spaces, receiving over two million visitors per year.

Instructional Services Team

The Tampa Library employs eight faculty librarians whose primary duties include library instruction, along with reference and research consultation services. This team includes the Assistant Director (AD) for Instructional Services who oversees the team and is responsible for providing vision, direction and training for the library faculty who teach. Since her arrival in 2012, the AD for Instructional Services has been working to reposition the library instruction team towards developing a more outcomes-based curriculum that was integrated more into the courses for which the library instruction was being given.

USF's AiA Team

The University of South Florida's Tampa Library was eager to become involved in the Assessment in Action (AiA) project. Our institutional team consisted of two librarians, two representatives from the First Year Composition team, and the university's director of the Academy for Teaching and Learning Excellence (ATLE). The latter provided invaluable insight and guidance for the team in the formulation of project goals and methodology.

Method Selection

Since arriving at the USF library in December of 2012, and inspired by the *The Value of Academic Libraries: A Comprehensive Research Review and Report*,[1] our team was very interested in engaging in an assessment project that would demonstrate the impact of library instruction on the academic achievement of students. This project was something that the instruction team sought to accomplish whether or not we were accepted into the AiA program. We had been thinking about it for some time and wanted to devise some kind of study that could link library instruction to academic achievement. We also wanted to transform our program into an outcomes-based, responsive curriculum that not only demonstrated student learning, but was also a thoughtful, integrated set of learning objectives that worked with the individual assignments students were completing rather than a "show-and-tell" of library resources and services. We chose to work with our First Year Composition team, housed within the Department of English. Our history of partnering with this group, along with our familiarity with the FYC curriculum made for a natural collaboration. Ultimately, we formulated the following research question: "Do First Year Composition students who attend information literacy instruction perform better on their assignments, or in their course than those who do not?"

The project began with an assessment of the currently available information. The USF Tampa Library has enjoyed a long-standing partnership with the First Year Composition (FYC) team and we were able to leverage that relationship to work out procedures for assessing the information literacy components already inherent in the FYC curriculum. The FYC team has maintained grade data for students for every semester since 2010 through the use of a standardized rubric. This rubric contains criteria that relate specifically to information literacy skills developed in tandem with the library. The students are evaluated on these skills as part of their overall grade for each project (of which there are three). Additionally, the library kept records of those classes that scheduled a face-to-face library instruction session, recording the course number and the name of the instructor. With access to this information, we decided to perform a secondary data analysis to determine if the student experience at a library instructional session had an impact on student success. We defined student success in terms of the number of points awarded to the student in the FYC assignment grading rubric.

Secondary analysis can be defined as "a type of research in which data collected by others are reanalyzed."[2] In this case, we selected two separate datasets. One data set was the student grade information gathered by the FYC team for the purposes of identifying trends in student learning. The other data set was the instruction scheduling information that the library maintains for the purposes of instruction program statistics. The main focus of the study involved the reconciliation of individual student grade data as recorded in the FYC grading rubric with his or her participation (or lack of) in information literacy instruction sessions going back one academic year. Because the data was readily available and had been recorded as a matter of organizational operations for some time, the team's research question and methodology seemed a natural, almost serendipitous, convergence of circumstances that allowed us to proceed with our investigation.

Limitations

Although the study method was obvious, the nature of the available data was not without issues. Indeed, upon further investigation into the library's instruction session data, it became obvious quickly that the data set was not particularly "clean," meaning there were numerous errors and inconsistencies in the data recording procedures. When instructors filled out the online form to request a library instruction session, the form allowed for a great deal of variation in field inputs. Therefore, some course numbers were recorded as standard course numbers, while others were simply recorded as "Composition" or "English". Without knowing the course number and section, a great deal of time was spent trying to resolve the identity of the course in question using the instructor's name, the day and time of the session, and the university's historical online course information system. Complicating matters was the practice of the Composition Department to record the program coordinator's name as the default instructor in cases where an instructor to teach the course had not yet been secured prior to the deadline for recording the course and section in the university's course information system. In some cases, it was impossible to determine the identity of the course that scheduled a library instruction session. In such cases, the course was discarded and not included in the analysis. In all, there were seven courses whose identities could not be ascertained.

Furthermore, because the data was historical in nature, and the library instruction curriculum at the time lacked any kind of uniformity or outcomes-based learning design, there was no assurance that the students who did receive library instruction all experienced the same type of instruction. As a result, there was no way to be confident that the any of the results showing a difference between the groups could be attributed to the efficacy of the instruction.

Project Implementation and AiA

Although we had a well-formulated research question and a corresponding methodology, it was our participation in the Assessment in Action (AiA) program that helped us develop crucial competencies in the areas of assessment documentation and communication to stakeholders that held the key to the success of the project. In particular, the AiA cohort to which our team was assigned was the single-most important factor in our ability to develop and complete our project. This group served as sounding-board and support partners who provided (within the AiA framework) well-reasoned and objective criticism that improved our efforts.

Using both data sets from FYC and library instruction session scheduling, we divided the FYC courses for the 2012 academic year into two groups: Those that scheduled a library instruction session and those that did not. Next, for each group, we averaged students' final grades as well as the average grade for the rubric criteria addressing information literacy. Using these averages, we ran an independent samples t-test to determine if there was a difference in the average grades of those students who attended library instruction versus those that did not.

The results indicated that students who participated in library instruction performed slightly better overall than those that did not. According to the test, the mean values between the two groups were consistent in key areas over three semesters, indicating that the students who attended a library instruction session received slightly higher grades in both the information literacy component, and overall in the class.

FIGURE 7.1. AVERAGE FINAL GRADE FOR STUDENTS ATTENDING LIBRARY INSTRUCTION VS. NON-ATTENDEES

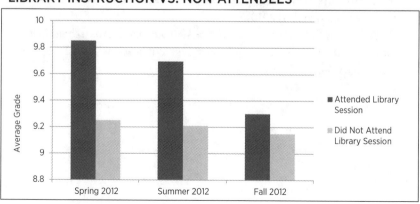

Suggestions & Recommendations

Since this study utilized a secondary analysis of two different data sets, it lacked a control group. As a result, there is still some question whether the appearance of statistical significance in the study is actually valid. Plans are in the works to design a follow-up study using a quasi-experimental design in which instructors are recruited for participation and instructional interventions are uniformly designed and administered. After a period of reflection at the conclusion of the study, and with the helpful insight of our AiA cohort, our team concluded that while our study was an excellent starting point, a more rigorous and thoughtfully designed study would yield more reliable information.

More importantly, however, we developed a stronger and more collaborative alliance with our FYC team whose participation, interest, and enthusiasm proved indispensable to the success of our project. The relationship between the library and a university's composition program is a natural one, and one that should be easy to cultivate if yours is nascent. We feel that our association with our composition program has been strengthened by our AiA project, and would recommend that any library seeking an assessment partnership look to such a group as an essential ally in an effort to demonstrate the value and impact that a library can have on student success.

Notes

1. Megan Oakleaf,. *The Value of Academic Libraries: A Comprehensive Research Review and Report* (Chicago, IL: Association of College & Research Libraries, 2010), http://www.ala.org/ala/mgrps/divs/acrl/issues/value/val_report. pdf (accessed March 1, 2013).

2. W. Paul Vogt, *Dictionary of Statistics & Methodology: A Nontechnical Guide for the Social Sciences* (Thousand Oaks: Sage Publications, Inc., 2005), s.v. "Secondary Analysis."

CHAPTER 8

Information Literacy Learning in First Year Composition:

A Rubric-Based Approach to Assessment

Robin E. Miller

University of Wisconsin-Eau Claire
millerob@uwec.edu

MORE THAN 2,000 UNDERGRADUATE students at the University of Wisconsin-Eau Claire (UW-Eau Claire) enroll annually in a first year composition course known as the Blugold Seminar for Critical Reading and Writing. While each instructor selects a theme or broad topic, all Blugold Seminars foster an inquiry-based, writing-intensive experience. They also share many of the same reading and writing assignments and emphasize the same course goals: Rhetorical Knowledge, Inquiry and Research, Writing Craft, and Digital Literacy.[1]

The Blugold Seminar was developed by UW-Eau Claire's Director of Composition and colleagues from the English Department. The course represents a departure for English faculty who had previously taught first year writing without a common curriculum. The course also represented a departure for library faculty—in 2010 library and English faculty began a multi-year collaboration to revise the library's approach to teaching information literacy (IL) in first year writing classrooms.[2] Developed over the course of several semesters, the revised IL lesson plan is now a standard learning experience integrated intentionally into the third segment of the Blugold Seminar course in which students complete an exploratory research assignment. Library faculty support more than 100 Blugold Seminar sections annually by teaching the one-shot IL instruction lesson developed in collaboration with the Composition Program. Writing instructors have the option of incorporating supplementary IL lessons and activities into their courses including specially developed videos, Lib-Guides, classroom lessons on trustworthy sources, and mini-visits from librarians who discuss topics like source evaluation and concept mapping. The library also provides an annual professional development workshop for composition instructors, introducing IL concepts and skills. Integrating IL instruction into the foundation first year composition course taken by most UW-Eau Claire students is strategically important because UW-Eau Claire emphasizes high impact practices like mentored undergraduate research experiences.

The library's IL lesson has been a standard experience for Blugold Seminar students since the 2011-2012 academic year. Since the launch of the new lesson librarians believe they have observed greater engagement among students and improved communication between instructor and student about the link between library instruction and the exploratory research assignment. After teaching the new Blugold Seminar IL lesson for a few years librarians at UW-Eau Claire were on the hunt for an authentic assessment method. The library has experimented with a variety of assessment techniques in first year composition with mixed results and varying response rates, including surveys of students and instructors and classroom assessment techniques (CATs). While we always appreciated largely positive responses from the self-selecting pool of respondents, the data gathered by means of this method has never provided an opportunity to take action. In our discussions of assessment we always returned to one key issue: without evaluating the artifacts of student research conducted following IL instruction how can we know what students are really learning from us? We knew we had a great opportunity to assess IL learning on a large scale as we were delivering the same instructional content across more than 100 sections of 15-20 students each.

Assessment in Action Program

UW-Eau Claire's acceptance into the first class of Assessment in Action (AiA) institutions enabled us to thoroughly explore assessment of first year writing. Ultimately AiA led us to develop a rubric in order to assess three key qualities of IL learning: evaluation of information, communication of evidence, and attribution. Our project examined two different artifacts of student learning using our rubric. One was an exploratory research assignment completed following information literacy instruction with a librarian and the other was a learning reflection completed at the end of the semester.

In the 2013/2014 academic year we collected 200 exploratory research assignments from a random selection of Blugold Seminar students. Each exploratory research assignment was reviewed and scored twice by members of an assessment team. The team consisted of four library faculty and four English faculty, who participated first in two norming sessions in order to achieve inter-rater reliability.

After the 200 exploratory research assignments were scored the AiA team leader accessed the learning reflections prepared by the same students whose exploratory assignments had been reviewed. Each learning reflection was examined to determine whether students had identified IL as a goal they met as part of their Blugold Seminar course.

Accessing both artifacts was possible because Blugold Seminar students upload their assignments to a digital portfolio database maintained in SharePoint. Portfolios are assigned student identification numbers but reviewers do not have access to additional information about the authors. This system was developed in order to facilitate several assessment projects undertaken by the Composition Program; UW-Eau Claire's AiA project was fortunate to benefit from the infrastructure.

Choice of Method

UW-Eau Claire's AiA research was guided by the question, "Do first year composition students learn when librarians collaborate with writing faculty to introduce information literacy concepts?" Rubric-style assessment was selected for this project because we wanted to examine the artifacts of student research, in this case written essays and multimedia works created in response to an exploratory research assignment. Rather than developing a rubric tool in a vacuum the AiA team adapted a rubric developed first at Carleton College[3] and later adapted by librarians at the Claremont Colleges.[4] We chose to adapt the Carleton rubric because we believed we would be able to locate those qualities in the products of student research at UW-Eau Claire.

Operationalizing the Inquiry Question

To the extent that student learning can be ascertained through artifacts of research and reflection we believe our two-pronged method related well to our research question. Using a rubric appealed to the AiA team leader because it establishes objective criteria which can be applied to a variety of artifacts giving a "clear measure of the level of the learning attained by the student."[5] Rubrics offer educators the opportunity to agree upon values that will be assessed; when properly normed, well-designed rubrics can ensure consistent scoring; and rubrics enable evaluators to collect rich, descriptive data.[6] Rubrics can also be designed to assess more than one quality, rather than assigning a single overall score to each student,[7] enabling our AiA team to score student performance in multiple relevant areas: evaluation of information, communication of evidence, and attribution.

We deepened our understanding of student learning by examining the end-of-semester reflection essays written by the students whose research artifacts had been scored. These reflections are authored in response to a prompt in which students must identify a course goal (or goals) which they believe they have achieved and explain why. Thirty percent of authors indicated that they believed they had achieved IL during their semester in the Blugold Seminar. These authors also achieved higher rubric scores than their peers who did not identify IL as an achieved course goal. This unexpected finding validated the extra work of correlating reflections to research assignment scores and pointed to a potentially intriguing meta-cognitive benefit of reflecting on one's own learning.

Limitations

Using a rubric to assess assignments given by a wide variety of instructors is risky because there are no guarantees that the qualities one hopes to score will be evident in every artifact of student learning. Rubrics are living documents however and can be revised as needed. For example looking to the future of this inquiry, UW-Eau Claire's rubric may drop attribution as a scored element. Attribution is surprisingly difficult to norm and we have found that we learn more from how students score in the realm of information evaluation.

The rubric assessment of student composition is time consuming. Adaptation and revision of the rubric, followed by the assembly of the assessment team and norming of the rubric took more than two months. After the rubric was normed and finalized inter-rater pairs of library and English faculty applied it to each randomly selected artifact of student research. The four librarians involved in reviewing student research were less experienced at reading and evaluating student work, lengthening the time each librarian spent reviewing and scoring artifacts.

Because rubric assessment is a lengthy process it was necessary to use a 10% sample of the exploratory research assignments authored by students in academic year 2013-2014. Thus we have not gathered data from every student engaged in the library's information literacy lesson. However, this project was designed to continue for several years. Three hundred and sixty artifacts will be scored in June 2015, representing about 15% of exploratory research assignments authored in the 2014-2015 academic year. Over time the bank of data about student information literacy learning will grow.

Implementation of the Method

UW-Eau Claire's AiA experience was truly collaborative. The project was designed and implemented by AiA team leader Robin Miller, Assistant Professor and Research & Instruction Librarian; Dr. Shevaun Watson, Associate Professor of English and Director of Composition; and Dr. Jennifer Fager, Director of University Assessment. Dr. Watson was instrumental in project design, offering essential insights about what we could realistically learn (and not learn) from student research conducted in the Blugold Seminar. In contrast to the librarians involved in the project Dr. Watson has extensive experience with performance evaluation using rubrics and with the norming process. She facilitated the norming sessions that ensured inter-rater reliability. Dr. Fager provided invaluable advice during the process of adapting and revising the rubric and planning the norming session.

Suggestions about Using Rubrics

Like any assessment tool, a rubric must be well-designed in order to be used for the collection of valid data. UW-Eau Claire chose to adapt the pre-existing Carlton College rubric to meet our local needs, to clarify concepts for the multi-disciplinary evaluation team, and to ensure that the AiA and evaluator teams were acting based on the same expectations of student learning.

To collect valid data with a rubric assessment teams must go through a norming process.[8] Librarians creating rubrics for student learning assessment would do well to ignore the impulse to "just skip the norming session." Norming sessions are work, but planning for and holding a norming session (or several, if necessary) ensures collection of valid data. These sessions require a facilitator, sample artifacts, and a rubric that may be adjusted because of discussions by session participants. The outcome of the norming session should be greater confidence in the rubric as an assessment tool and in the team of people applying it to student work.

Rubrics are an excellent tool for assessing student performance. However, the simpler the rubric the better. They must feature a simple set of criteria that all evaluators understand. While eliminating subjectivity is probably impossible, authors of rubrics should be mindful of adjectives and subjective phrases with relative meanings. Rubrics with wide scoring scales are difficult apply reliably, so keeping the scale at one through four or one through three is advisable.

Be sure that your rubric truly reflects stakeholder values. During the development process, your colleagues may reveal interests that align well with the rubric or that should be pursued using another method or tool. While a rubric can be used to assess many qualities at once, the scope of the rubric should be limited to ensure it is being used to collect measurable data.

Alternatives to Rubrics

The AiA project at UW-Eau Claire utilized rubrics because we had access to the artifacts of student research assigned after an IL instruction session. Librarians at UW-Eau Claire are not the instructors of record in any composition class and we lack the option to create and grade a separate assignment which could be used to capture student IL learning (for example a

Classroom Assessment Technique like a pre-/post-test, a worksheet, or a quick writing assignment). In addition, we believe that we collected the most holistic view of student IL learning possible because we applied a valid research tool (the rubric) to the artifacts of student research and followed up by reviewing student reflections on their own learning. This was a relatively complex method but it enabled our AiA team to collect data authentic to the student experience with research and inquiry in the Blugold Seminar.

Conclusion

While rubric-based assessment is both time consuming and complex, library faculty at UW-Eau Claire were able to use this tool to better understand the work students do after IL instruction. Combining this approach with reflective writing offered unique insights about what students believe they achieve versus what they actually achieve in the realm of information literacy.

The Assessment in Action program jumpstarted a series of library assessment initiatives at UW-Eau Claire. Because AiA requires extensive collaboration between the library and campus partners, UW-Eau Claire's project deepened our relationship with the Composition Program and fostered new learning opportunities for the AiA team leader, team members, and library faculty. AiA's professional development opportunities introduced invaluable assessment concepts which UW-Eau Claire is implementing in a variety of new projects.

Notes

1. Shevaun Watson, "Blugold Seminar for Critical Reading and Writing," University of Wisconsin-Eau Claire, accessed May 1, 2015, http://www.uwec.edu/Blugoldseminar/index.htm

2. Shevaun Watson, Cathy Rex, Jill Markgraf, Hans Kishel, Eric Jennings and Kate Hinnant, "Revising the 'One-shot' through Lesson Study: Collaborating with Writing Faculty to Rebuild a Library Instruction Session," *College and Research Libraries* 74, no. 4 (2013): 384–388; Jill Markgraf, Kate Hinnant, Eric Jennings and Hans Kishel, *Maximizing the One-Shot: Connecting Library Instruction with the Curriculum* (Lanham, MD: Rowman & Littlefield, 2015).

3. Iris Jastram, Danya Leebaw and Heather Tompkins, "Situating Information Literacy within the Curriculum: Using a Rubric to Shape a Program," *portal: Libraries and the Academy* 14, no. 2 (2014): 165–86.

4. Char Booth, M. Sara Lowe, Natalie Tagge and Sean M. Stone, "Degrees of Impact: Analyzing the Effects of Progressive Librarian Course Collaborations on Student Performance," *College & Research Libraries*, 76, no. 5 (2015): 623–651; M. Sara Lowe, Natalie Tagge and Sean M. Stone, "Librarian Impact on Student Information Literacy Skills in First-Year Seminar Programs," *portal: Libraries and the Academy*, 15, no. 3 (2015): 489–512.

5. Karen R. Diller and Sue F. Phelps, "Learning Outcomes, Portfolios, and Rubrics, Oh My! Authentic Assessment of an Information Literacy Program," *portal: Libraries and the Academy* 8, no. 1 (2008): p. 78.

6. Megan Oakleaf, "Dangers and Opportunities: A Conceptual Map of Information Literacy Assessment Approaches," *portal: Libraries and the Academy* 8, no. 3 (2008), pp. 244–247, accessed May 1, 2015, http://meganoakleaf.info/dangersopportunities.pdf

7. Mark Emmons and Wanda Martin, "Engaging Conversation: Evaluating the Contribution of Library Instruction to the Quality of Student Research," *College and Research Libraries* 63, no. 6 (2002), p. 549.

8. Claire Holmes and Megan Oakleaf, "The Official (and Unofficial) Rules for Norming Rubrics Successfully," *Journal of Academic Librarianship* 39, no. 6 (2013): 599–602.

CHAPTER 9

Comparing Apples and Oranges:

Putting Virginia Tech's FYE Inquiry Assessment Program into Perspective

Kyrille Goldbeck DeBose

Virginia Polytechnic Institute and State University
kdebose@vt.edu

Carolyn Meier

Virginia Polytechnic Institute and State University
cmeier@vt.edu

BEFORE 2010 VIRGINIA TECH did not have a formalized First Year Experience (FYE) program. Instead each department offered a general introductory course for their majors or as a part of the general educational curriculum. Students also had the opportunity to join several residential learning communities. While this approach had been satisfactory in the past, when the Southern Association of Colleges and Schools (SACS) Commission on Colleges (COS) conducted their accreditation review in 2009 one of their recommendations was for Virginia Tech to incorporate a centrally administered FYE program as part of a Quality Enhancement Plan (QEP). Administration quickly established a team to work on a five-year program to implement an FYE program in which all colleges would participate. As many of the introductory courses were subject-based, during initial discussions colleges and departments indicated they did not want the FYE course to be an extended orientation program. Instead they wanted the FYE classes to focus on developing students' professional and subject expertise in their area of study in addition to promoting academic success. Additionally it would be at the discretion of the college to determine if the FYE course would be offered as a college- or department-level course, as well as if it would be a requirement for all incoming and/or transfer students. The delivery method of the course would be determined by course leaders whether online-only, in-person-only, or a hybrid model of instruction. Some courses would be lead by instructors while other would have various levels of faculty involvement with students grouped with peer mentors.

In spite of the many different ways the course could be offered, college and departmental representatives identified three areas of student growth to be incorporated in every FYE course: Problem-solving, inquiry, and integration. Incorporating these areas of focus often involved making significant changes to the content of the original "intro" classes. The FYE office developed a series of grants for departments or colleges that provided the monetary support for implementing required changes. Applications were reviewed on an annual basis and funding was allocated according to alignment with the three programmatic outcomes. All courses would incorporate the Virginia Tech Common book*, include a section on advising, and a partnership with the Student Affairs department. Campus partners were often involved the problem-solving and integration components of the course, but the inquiry piece required a librarian's inclusion on the planning team. To enforce this particular partnership each FYE proposal included the signature of the librarian working with the course instructors to develop the inquiry portion of course materials. The librarian was responsible for tailoring the inquiry materials to the needs of the discipline.

The next challenge was to identify an assessment tool that would be implemented across all programs. The tool needed to work across disciplines, pedagogies, levels of librarian involvement, and differing types of student engagement. Because of the large number of students involved, a standardized instrument for assessment needed to have an established delivery method, facilitate quick grading, and incorporate an easy method

---

* For more information about this program, see http://www.commonbook.vt.edu/

of data collection. The assessment would need to demonstrate the positive or negative impact of a programmatic change for each FYE course. This would provide instructors with useful data in deciding whether to pursue the implemented change or return to the previous method of inquiry delivery. Additionally the Office of First Year Experiences dictated that any inquiry assessment tool would be implemented and administered by the Office of Assessment and Evaluation (OAE). The OAE was tasked with storing the data, assisting program leaders with interpreting the results of the assessment tool's application, and tracking student improvement for each cohort that went through an FYE program.

Librarians were not originally included in the inquiry assessment discussions. However as the OAE prepared to begin actual development they realized they were unsure of where to begin, other than knowing that the instrument format would be multiple choice. Realizing that inquiry revolves around information literacy, the OAE contacted one of our librarians for help and a partnership was formed; librarians were unaware at the time of how this partnership would impact their instruction and their place in the university community. The group tasked with formulating the assessment tool explored currently available information literacy evaluation tools but quickly decided none directly addressed Virginia Tech's specific outcomes. The group decided an in-house assessment tool was needed that utilized multiple-choice questions in the form of pre- and post-tests in order gather data on student growth.

Questions were divided in two main areas: *accessing and evaluating information*, and *using information ethically*. The *accessing and evaluating information* section featured questions covering information types, searching strategies, reading citations, and web evaluation. Questions in the *using information ethically* section addressed the need for citations, common knowledge, and in-text citations. Questions on the pre-test were purposely general whereas some on the post-test were specifically designed to evaluate knowledge of particular Virginia Tech resources.

Five FYE programs constituted the first cohort in the fall of 2010. We piloted our newly created assessment tool, the Information Literacy Test (ILT), among this group. Our main goal was to ascertain growth in inquiry skills across a variety of programs but initially we were also concerned about the reliability of the questions. Students were asked to take a pre-test during the first two weeks of the semester. The post-test was released four weeks before the semester's end. The range of improvement registered between the pre- and post-tests varied considerably with each program. With such a small sample size however it was impossible to determine if this variation was attributable to the actual library instruction or some flaw in the ILT questions.

In the fall of 2011 eight more FYE programs were granted funding which allowed us to try out the pre- and post-tests once again. The growth in the number of programs provided the opportunity to examine trends across a larger population size. This helped us determine if the variation in the previous analyses were attributable to the assessment tool itself or if the discrepancies were based on other factors. In the summer of 2012, using the results of both sets of tests, librarians teaching in the FYE courses were asked to map their curriculum to the ILT questions. This included examining:

- how the inquiry instruction was delivered in the course, including:
  — the number of times the librarian met with the class (one-shot or multiple sessions)
  — how much time the librarian was given to teach in the given session(s)
  — how the interactions with students took place (solely in person, solely online, flipped classroom)
  — what specific inquiry skills were being taught in the course (e.g. Boolean, services, search strategies, etc.)
- what exercises were utilized in and outside of the inquiry-based session(s)
- how the inquiry piece related to the problem-solving and/or integration projects

A comparison of the content of the inquiry sessions and the questions posed in the ILT assessment tool allowed us to identify the commonalities and discrepancies between skills taught and outcomes tested. We discovered instances in which a question on a specific skill was answered correctly in only one or two courses. In these cases we took one of two actions. We either changed the question so as to be applicable across the disciplines, or the skill was incorporated into the other courses. A valid indication of student growth is only attainable if all students are exposed to the same basic content. Otherwise how could students that were not exposed to a particular skill could be expected to demonstrate a marked growth in comprehension and utilization of that skill? This curriculum alignment process is conducted on a regular basis to ensure standard instructional practice that meets programmatic outcomes.

As the partnership between the FYE course leaders and librarians grew stronger a few librarians became involved in analyzing the qualitative inquiry reflections in greater detail. When we received the ILT post-test data from the 2012 cohort we discovered a significant discrepancy between the scores and what students had written in their reflections. Students could correctly answer the multiple choice questions concerning ethics on the post-test, but when we asked them to articulate their experiences in a reflective writing piece it became apparent that many could not put the ethical knowledge covered in the course into practice. Additional conversations with the English Composition faculty revealed the same disconnect. To address this problem in fall 2013 we added a series of reflective questions to the ILT post-test. The inclusion of open-ended questions provided a way to gather additional data within the tool itself regarding student growth and the ability (or inability) to apply the inquiry practices taught in the course.

Analyzing the data from the three cohorts drove home the fact that each discipline uses its own terminology and language to describe components of inquiry skills. For example primary sources are defined quite differently by the humanities and the sciences, respectively. In order to continue using the tool across multiple disciplines we adjusted the language and the examples used in the pre- and post-test questions. We also had to be vigilant in keeping the ILT up-to-date to reflect current inquiry teaching practices. In the fall of 2012 the University Libraries fully implemented Summon, a discovery layer, on top of their resources. This new service fundamentally changed how introductory library instruction courses were taught and questions in the ILT relating to Virginia Tech's library catalog had to be modified or removed.

In spite of the fact that pre- and post-tests became a fundamental part of courses including library instruction, we discovered in our first two years of testing that there were significantly fewer students taking the post-tests than the pre-tests. Conversations and observation eventually bore out that incoming students would often fill out the pre-test with no questions or hesitance, due in part we think to fresh enthusiasm and fewer competing interests, but by the end of the semester competing priorities edged out the post-test in importance. ITL post-test data were a crucial element for understanding the impact of acquired inquiry skills, so librarians leveraged their partnerships with instructors to make the post-test a graded course component. This provided sufficient incentive for students to complete the post-test.

While creating and utilizing the assessment tool had its highs and lows, all involved would gladly do it again. There have been so many positive lessons. We have gained valuable data about student learning and how our teaching practices impact their comprehension. One of the major takeaways involved the value of being willing to take a risk and possibly make mistakes. The process of aligning curriculum with an assessment tool was a new and instructive experience. We learned the wisdom of starting small in order to gain large rewards. Partnerships are not built overnight but strengthened over time, so rather than pushing into content areas we have used the data to articulate the value of inquiry sessions. With the support of strong partnerships new and different pedagogies can be explored and analyzed. Unsurprisingly, the creation of an assessment tool in-house requires a great deal of work, testing, and vigilance, but ownership of the tool allows for greater customization and flexibility. It is vital to involve people from different disciplines in a major assessment project in order to ensure quality. Field-testing takes time and even after an instrument has been verified a yearly review will be necessary to ensure questions are still valid.

Over the course of the past five years we have not been surprised to see as more librarians became involved with teaching the inquiry component of FYE courses that relationships with their respective academic departments have gotten stronger. Several librarians have become mentors to others taking on new FYE courses, expanding the collaborative network even beyond departmental borders to include campus partners such as the Office of First Year Experiences and Office of Assessment and Evaluation. Each group continues striving to incorporate more meaningful and impactful teaching methods designed to promote the development of inquiry skills as an integral part of students' academic progress. In spite of its limitations we have found the ILT to be a valuable tool in assessing the degree to which inquiry skills have been successfully addressed in each FYE program.

Further Reading

Bain, Ken. *What the Best College Teachers Do.* Cambridge, Mass.: Harvard University Press, 2004.

Booth, Char. *Reflective Teaching, Effective Learning Instructional Literacy for Library Educators.* Chicago: American Library Association, 2011.

Brown, Peter C. *Make It Stick: The Science of Successful Learning.* Cambridge, Mass.: Belknap Press of Harvard University Press, 2014

Duke, Lynda M. *College Libraries and Student Culture: What We Now Know.* Chicago: American Library Association, 2011.

Hardesty, Larry L. *The Role of the Library in the First College Year.* Columbia, SC: National Resource Center for the First-Year Experience & Students in Transition, University of South Carolina, 2007.

CHAPTER 10

Assessment in Action Case Study:

Do Online Learning Modules Have a Role in Information Literacy Instruction?

Henri Mondschein

Pearson Library, California Lutheran University
mondsche@callutheran.edu

HOW CAN ACADEMIC LIBRARIANS engage undergraduate students and infuse fresh active learning approaches that enhance learning during the delivery of information literacy (IL) instruction? Does adding in-class tutorials to library instruction sessions positively impact student learning of IL concepts? This Assessment in Action (AiA) action research project addressed these pressing concerns and explored this contemporary and practical problem in library instruction. In the broader realm of assessment, the project tackled some of the challenges of assessing student learning when online tutorials and brief quizzes were added to a 50-minute instruction session. The study employed a mixed study design, blending basic quantitative techniques with qualitative approaches. The qualitative responses from the students provided the most fruitful assessment data in the form of open-ended responses that evolved into themes indicating how the participants reacted to the tutorials. These responses provided rich feedback on how the tutorials might be improved. Additionally, the project outcomes offer practical guidelines for instruction librarians interested in incorporating information literacy tutorials into their practice.

The combination of in-class tutorials with built-in quizzes designed around the ACRL standards and learning outcomes can potentially reinforce learning through activities fostering active-learning and student engagement.[1] Quizzes can also be used to assess student learning of IL concepts.

The design and creation of three online tutorials was central to the project and these addressed the concepts of evaluation of information and using information responsibly. A goal was to scaffold or sequence learning across the three tutorials. First-year students were introduced to basic concepts on evaluating sources and plagiarism while sophomores, juniors, and seniors explored more advanced concepts including the critical evaluation of research studies, fair use, and copyright. In adapting Bloom's Taxonomy, the project team designed each tutorial to coincide with these skills:

First Year: Knowledge

Sophomore/Junior: Comprehension

Senior/Capstone: Application/Synthesis

The project team also considered how IL tutorials can be implemented in class instruction. One way is to complement instruction by having students work through an online learning activity and reinforce learning with brief quizzes embedded in the tutorials. The instruction librarian can then highlight topics covered in the tutorial and review the quiz questions in a discussion format. Likewise, the tutorials can be used in a flipped classroom setting. The course professor can assign the tutorials as homework prior to the library session. In this context, the instruction librarian can focus on reinforcing the tutorial concepts and emphasize discussion and active learning activities.

Turning to the specifics of the project, the study participants consisted of 74 undergraduate students from a convenience sample who were enrolled in eight undergraduate courses during the fall 2013 semester at a private liberal arts university. The sample consisted of 77% freshmen, 10% sophomores, 5.7% juniors, and 7% seniors. Courses included biology, business, criminal justice, freshman English, exercise science, and sociology. Because a key objective involved the assessment of student learning, a small research study was designed enabling empirical data to be collected and analyzed. More specifically, the project team set out to determine if combining online tutorials with information literacy instruction enhanced learning. The design of the study involved two groups of students; one group receiving a traditional instructional session and a second group receiving an instructional session and an online tutorial. Baseline levels of student information literacy skills for both groups were measured with an information literacy skills assessment before they were exposed to the library instructional session and tutorial. Information literacy skills were measured again for both groups at the end of the semester using the same assessment.

A test was identified and used with the permission of Amy Catalano of Hofstra University in New York. Catalano adapted the *Beile Test of Information Literacy for Education (B-TILED)*[2] in her own work and expanded the scope of the test from focusing on information literacy skills of education students to a broader undergraduate population.

Multiple choice items measured ACRL standards One, Two, Three and Five. However, because the focus of the tutorials and the study were on evaluating information (Standard Three) and using information ethically and legally (Standard Five), two subscales were further refined and results focused on those specific standards:

- Evaluation subscale: Six items (e.g. "You must write a paper on the environmental practices of Sony Corporation. Which of the following is most likely to provide balanced information?")
- Responsibility subscale: Seven items (e.g. "When is it ethical to use the ideas of another person in a research paper?")

Classes were selected using a convenience sample and assigned to either an experimental or control group. Preliminary analyses from a quantitative perspective assessed students in the tutorial group only and consisted of two paired-sample t-tests to assess for differences between pre- and post-tests for ACRL Standard Three (Evaluation) and ACRL Standard Five (Responsibility). Results trended toward support of the hypothesis, in which adding in-class tutorials and quizzes to 50-minute information literacy sessions reinforced learning of information literacy concepts and showed potential for engaging learners by providing an active learning activity. Overall, the results showed improvements in scores, although not at a level of significance. Limitations of this research include a very small sample size, data from only the tutorial group, and use of a convenience sample, which limits the generalizability to a larger population. Further research and analysis will assess differences in how the two groups of students perform. Nevertheless, these preliminary findings suggest that the tutorials may have a positive impact on student learning of ACRL Standards Three and Five.

While the quantitative data provided some evidence of student learning, the qualitative responses provided valuable insight about student experiences with the tutorials. Overall, open-ended responses indicated that students preferred completing the learning modules in class as part of a library session as opposed to outside of class. An interesting finding that contradicts the current movement of "flipped classes" suggests that students appear to prefer the integration of online tutorials with instruction.

Also, the students participating in the study had a voice in shaping the recommendations coming from the research by providing reactions to their overall experiences with the tutorials. These responses produced qualitative themes, which in turn, emerged as practical feedback for enhancing the tutorials. The broader qualitative themes included format, engagement, relevance, incentives, and delivery. Some of the practical examples distilled from the broader themes included repurposing the tutorials by creating shorter versions; using the tutorials with the university's first-year experience program; targeting the senior-level tutorial in capstone research classes and integrating the tutorials in flipped instructions sessions. Rich qualitative data is a strong advantage of using a mixed-methods design in an assessment project of this scope. In general, the quantitative results provided the data and *evidence* for student learning, while the qualitative results revealed how students *experienced* the tutorials.

Furthermore, as action research, this project enabled the librarian/team leader to become a participant-observer in some key ways both in the design of digital learning objects or tutorials and in the delivery of the instruction and in performing the research. A highlight of the project was the formation of an effective community of inquiry consisting of the project team, teaching faculty, and students. In addition, all contributed in unique ways. The teaching faculty were afforded an opportunity to observe a new model for teaching information literacy, while students provided valuable feedback for designing learner-centered tutorials. The project team included three campus members who were able to bring unique perspectives and knowledge to the project. A colleague from the Center for Teaching and Learning offered unique perspective on instructional design, digital learning objects and communication research methodology. A second team member was the director of the educational effectiveness department. His input on assessment kept the focus of the project on the big picture—student learning and the information literacy student learning outcome. The third team member was an adjunct psychology professor with expertise in research methodology and quantitative analysis. She provided assistance with importing survey results into SPSS, selecting statistical tests, analysis and with interpretation of the results.

As a team venture, the project afforded all campus team members opportunities to work together toward a common goal—the success of the project and furthering student learning. Central to creating a positive team experience is respecting and acknowledging the workloads of all team members by assigning everyone meaningful tasks and showing that one is mindful of work responsibilities outside of the project.

The project also featured a unique collaborative effort of the campus team and an instruction design team at Credo Literati who worked with the team leader to create the tutorials. This required considerable virtual work during which story boards were created by the Credo team and reviewed by the team leader who in turn responded with edits and suggestions during each stage of the tutorial design process. As a team leader of an Assessment in Action project, one is well served by selecting a multi-disciplinary team where each team member can provide consultation and guidance in specific project areas.

In planning an assessment project, always anticipate potential problems. For example, it is vital to gain required consent before collecting data. One critical step is submitting all required forms to the campus Institutional Review Board (IRB). Always be sure to keep the IRB advised on any project changes. Even a minor change requires a revision to the original IRB application.

Sometimes, lack of cooperation from study participants can hinder progress. For example, while students were generally required to complete a pre-test and post-test during class, one group of students was asked to take the pre-test outside of class. Even though the entire class appeared eager to participate, only a couple of students actually completed the post-test. In subsequent classes, students were required to complete the pre-test during class with cooperation from the course professors. Nearly all participated. The lesson here is to administer tests or surveys during class whenever possible. Finally, incentives do work; ask the course instructor if students can receive a reward for participating. This can include bonus points or extra credit.

A number of tangible campus outcomes resulted from the work. Overall, the project was a bonus for generating information literacy assessment data. Because the pre-test and post-test focused on information literacy skills and concepts, the results provided evidence of student learning for these student learning outcomes, something that educational effectiveness and assessment departments appreciate coming from libraries. Next, the project shined the spotlight on the importance of active learning as a pedagogical method that must be woven into the fabric of today's undergraduate curriculum. Consequently, a decision was made to build the university's first active learning classroom in the library which features modular work spaces, white boards, and technology to support problem-based learning, small group work and similar forms of inquiry-based teaching and learning. The project spawned further collaboration and working partnerships among the team leader and members of the campus community, including an instructional designer with the university's Center for Teaching and Learning. This colleague repurposed and improved the original tutorials from the AiA study based on the student feedback. Additionally, faculty teaching first-year seminars are integrating the tutorials into their courses. Furthermore, the undergraduate core curriculum at the university will be reexamined and more active learning experiences, tutorials and digital learning objects will be considered as fundamental to a 21st Century undergraduate curriculum. Finally, the practical outcomes of this action research project can inform other institutions, libraries, and instruction librarians on effective ways to blend tutorials and digital learning objects with information literacy instruction.

Notes

1. Barbara A. Blummer and Olga Kritskaya, "Best Practices for Creating an Online Tutorial: A Literature Review," *Journal of Web Librarianship* 3, no. 3 (2009): 199–216, *ERIC*, EBSCO*host* (accessed May 31, 2015); Jennifer Holland, Erica DeFrain and Yvonne Mery, *The Survey of Best Practices in Developing Online Information Literacy Tutorials* (New York, NY: Primary Research Group, Inc., 2013); Karen Kate Kellum, Amy E. Mark and Debra A. Riley-Huff, "Development, Assessment and Use of an On-line Plagiarism

Tutorial," *Library Hi Tech* 29, no. 4 (November 2011): 641–654, *Library, Information Science & Technology Abstracts*, EBSCO*host* (accessed May 31, 2015); Susan L. Silver and Lisa T. Nickel, "Are Online Tutorials Effective? A Comparison of Online and Classroom Library Instruction Methods," *Research Strategies* 20, no. 4 (January 1, 2005): 389–396, *ERIC*, EBSCO*host* (accessed May 31, 2015); Sara Thornes, "Creating an Online Tutorial to Support Information Literacy and Academic Skills Development," *Journal of Information Literacy* 6, no. 1 (June 2012): 81–95, *Library Literature & Information Science Full Text (H.W. Wilson)*, EBSCO*host* (accessed May 31, 2015).

2. Penny M. Beile O'Neal, "Development and Validation of the Beile Test of Information Literacy for Education (B-TILED)" (doctoral dissertation, University of Central Florida, 2005), https://ezproxy.callutheran.edu/login?url=http://search.proquest.com/docview/305363702?accountid=9839

CHAPTER 11

Complementary, Not Conflicting Data:

Using Citation Analysis and NVivo to Explore Student Learning

Phil Jones

Grinnell College
jonesphi@grinnell.edu

HOW DO RESEARCH LITERACY sessions impact the quality of the sources students select and, more broadly, student learning? This question guided us as we began our Assessment in Action (AiA) project, but it, like the methods and tools we used, changed over the four semesters we have worked on the project.† Our AiA team met multiple times to consider potential research topics and relevant scholarly literature. Together we crafted the following question to focus and to lead our work: Following a research literacy session for classes in each of Grinnell College's three academic divisions, did students include more relevant, timely and authoritative sources in their revised bibliographies than in their draft bibliographies? This chapter includes reflection on the methods and tools used in our study, changes made as the project progressed and discussion of our preliminary findings.

To address our research question, we collaborated with faculty members from the Departments of Psychology (science division), Economics

---

† For a full discussion of our action research project, please see: Jones, Phil, Julia Bauder and Kevin Engel. "Mixed or Complementary Messages: Making the Most of Unexpected Assessment Results." *College & Research Libraries*. Forthcoming.

(social studies division) and Spanish (humanities division) to design an assignment for assessment. The assignment required students first to create draft bibliographies on their own and then revise their work following a research literacy session with a librarian. We decided to do a performance assessment of our students' sources which would provide us with a quantitative measure of actual student work involving research. (Please see Appendix A for a copy of our bibliography item rating form.)

By reviewing the scholarly literature of library science, we were reminded that for decades librarians have used citation analysis to study their students' sources. In most citation analysis studies, librarians rated students' sources, and sometimes faculty members did so. However we found no studies in which students rated their own work. Accordingly, our performance assessment called for three faculty members to rate the quality of the sources for only the students in their class, and for each student to rate the quality of their own sources. A total of forty students participated in our study.

Our initial review of the quantitative data showed that, based on their professor's ratings, students were doing a good job of selecting relevant and timely material. However, the faculty ratings for source authority dropped slightly on students' revised bibliographies. This latter result puzzled us, as did our finding that the students rated their revised source lists as less timely and authoritative than faculty.

Since we had collected qualitative data as part of this study, we decided to change the study's research design to a mixed-methods experimental one by adding a qualitative component to our quantitative performance assessment. These new qualitative data were the students' written responses to three questions included in their bibliography item rating form:

1. Did you omit any sources appearing in your draft bibliography from your revised bibliography? If so, why did you decide not to include those sources in your revised bibliography?
2. Of all of the sources in your bibliography, which single source has most influenced your thinking on the topic? Why did you find that particular source so influential?
3. What are two or three main points you learned from the research literacy session a librarian held with this class earlier in the semester?

We strove to ask questions not routinely included on end-of-session feedback forms. Rather we asked questions intended primarily to prompt students' reflection on their research processes and sources and, secondarily, to help students articulate what they learned from an instruction session. Students provided detailed written responses to these questions soon after submitting their revised bibliographies.

Previous to our study, we had no means of exploring how the often detailed, insightful statements students provided as session feedback related to the quality of the sources they cited in research papers, presentations or projects. Nvivo, a powerful qualitative data analysis tool, allowed us to run cross tabulations of these source ratings with the students' written responses. The process of learning and using Nvivo took a significant amount of time. We were fortunate however that one of our librarian AiA team members has expertise with the software. We also received early, invaluable guidance from the staff of DASIL, our campus' Data Analysis and Social Inquiry Lab.

To date, we have found little clear relationship between what students reported learning during a research literacy session and the professors' ratings of their students' sources. However our use of Nvivo prompted an intriguing question. Rather than trying to privilege one form of data over another, what could we learn by considering that these data were simply sending different, perhaps complementary messages? Our quantitative finding that the forty students in our study selected relatively strong sources prior to working with a librarian could be attributed to the fact that nearly all of these students had taken part in a research literacy session as first-semester students at Grinnell. In doing so they were well prepared for upper-division sessions such as conducted in this study. Additionally the fact that our students had questions about source authority and timeliness after working with a librarian might indicate that our research literacy sessions challenged the way the students' judged and selected sources for their academic work.

At present, we are more interested in discussing our findings with campus colleagues than in offering precise, clear cut results. We are pleased that our AiA project has created an opportunity for our full project team to meet again and discuss our work. It also is an opportunity for us to share and consider the significance of our project with groups across campus, such as Grinnell's librarians and assessment committee, as well as groups of faculty and academic departments.

We also considered our participation in the AiA program as an opportunity for our library to try a number of assessment projects we had been considering. Our hope was that doing so would bring assessment into our regular, ongoing work. To this end, our AiA team worked with circulation supervisors to track interlibrary loan use during an academic year, and with our institutional research office to compare that information to students' grade point average (GPA). We also compared students' book circulation histories, use of individual research consultations, and participation in research literacy sessions to metrics of academic success such as graduation rates and GPA. As these assessments progressed, however, our focus necessarily returned to the citation analysis project. We were not seeing clear trends in these ancillary assessment data and did not have the time to look more closely or to tweak these data collections or analyses.

In retrospect, we see that, like so many of the students we work with in classes, at the research desk or online, we were ambitious and so undertook too much assessment work along with an AiA research project, our priority. Our suggestion would be to start slowly and to expand the reach and sophistication of assessment work over time, to let an initial, focused project lead to the next research question rather than trying to investigate a range of questions from the outset.

We also found that as we began to review our AiA project data, additional calculations and intriguing research questions presented themselves to us. For instance, we calculated student, class and overall average ratings for each of our three source criteria. However, we did not calculate a single average combining these criteria. We realized late in our research process that this additional calculation would have been helpful, but by that time we were analyzing our quantitative and qualitative data with Nvivo. Unfortunately Nvivo, although sophisticated and robust, does not allow data sets to be edited once imported. We learned that as you undertake a research project it is impossible to anticipate which data will end up being the most meaningful and interesting. So, again, we were reminded of the importance of retaining focus and pursuing a reasonable, doable number of data points. We can explore any new ideas, questions or calculations the next time we assess our research literacy work. This way, we have reason to look forward to future assessment work. Throughout the course of our AiA project, we learned and grew as a team of researchers, but we were (and still are) a group of busy college faculty and professional staff. It seemed easy, perhaps even advisable, that some team members complete portions of our project work alone. Once working with our project data, both technical and nuanced, we were at first grateful when a team member undertook the bulk of the decision making and analysis. However, when we began to discuss and prepare a report on our project, we realized that team members had different ideas as to how key variables should be defined or calculations figured. We advise that teams work together on all phases of action research projects. The entire team should also acquire at least a working knowledge of the project design and data. In addition they should agree that the end result of an accurate, fully developed project is more important than meeting artificial deadlines.

In conclusion, our study was shaped as much by the practical realities of collaborating with a range of faculty and over three dozen students as it was by experimental design ideals. We had to make some compromises. If we were to do our study over again, there are two important points we would consider:

- Have students rate both their rough and revised bibliographies, as this may allow for fuller comparisons and more meaningful results.
- Have students and faculty members evaluate a source as it is actually used in a final research paper or project. The relevance, timeliness or authority of a source listed in a student's bibliography may not always be evident in situ. Rather, attention should be paid to how a source supports or advances a student's actual academic work.

Librarians often tell their students that academic research is recursive rather than linear. It is guided by a research question, which is itself likely to evolve as a topic, sources, data or findings change. It has been refreshing to learn that the advice we give our students holds true for our own research. Our action research project yielded two sets of rich, local data, both of which have the potential to challenge and improve our teaching and our students' learning.

APPENDIX A. Rating of Bibliography Items, Assessment in Action Project: Fall 2013

Student's name: _____

Professor's name: _____

Department and Course Number: _____

Please rate each item appearing on your final bibliography using the table below. If you would like to add additional information on any item, please do so at the bottom of the page.

CITATION:

THIS ITEM IS...	STRONGLY AGREE (5)	(4)	(3)	(2)	STRONGLY DISAGREE (1)
Very relevant to my topic					
Timely					
Authoritative					

Further Reading

Dykeman, Amy and Barbara King. "Term Paper Analysis: A Proposal for Evaluating Bibliographic Instruction." *Research Strategies* 1, no. 1 (1983): 14–21.

Gratch, Bonnie. "Toward a Methodology for Evaluating Research Paper Bibliographies." *Research Strategies* 3, no. 4 (1985): 170–177.

Hovde, Karen. "Check the Citation: Library Instruction and Student Paper Bibliographies." *Research Strategies* 17, no. 1 (Spring, 2000): 3–9.

Knight-Davis, Stacey and Jan S. Sung. "Analysis of Citations in Undergraduate Papers." *College & Research Libraries* 69, no. 5 (September 01, 2008): 447–458.

Long, Casey M. and Milind M. Shrikhande. "Using Citation Analysis to Evaluate and Improve Information Literacy Instruction." In *Collaborative Information Literacy Assessment: Strategies for Evaluating Teaching and Learning*, edited by Thomas P. Mackey and Trudi E. Jacobson, 5. New York: Neal-Schuman Publishers, Inc., 2010.

Portmann, Chris A. and Adrienne Julius Roush. "Assessing the Effects of Library Instruction." *The Journal of Academic Librarianship* 30, no. 6 (11, 2004): 461–465.

CHAPTER 12

Predictors of Information Literacy Competencies at a Large University:
A Reflection on Testing Methods

Amy Catalano

Hofstra University
amy.catalano@hofstra.edu

HOFSTRA UNIVERSITY, LOCATED ON Long Island, NY, regularly assesses student learning, engagement, and satisfaction through multiple avenues of data collection, including Institutional Research, and on the department/program level. Information literacy (IL) assessment had been conducted not only by the library but by a committee in the College of Liberal Arts and Sciences. Further, the university's commitment to developing information literate students is clearly articulated in the mission statement.[1] Assessment activities already implemented at the library level tended to be reactive in nature, however. That is, they were embedded in the final exams or presented during "one-shot" assignment-based classes right after instruction. So, they really only captured short-term teaching quality, at best, and the strength one's memory. As the goal of the Assessment in Action (AiA) initiative is to investigate the value of academic libraries, our initial inquiry involved exploring how the library's instruction contributes to the overall development and retention of IL skills on campus in a more objective way than we had done previously.[2] We also investigated whether or not, how much and what type of library instruction impacted the IL skills. Toward that end, a validated IL test was administered to a large sample that included students from many majors, at different levels, who had and had not received various types of library instruction. Because librarians at our institution believe that imparting information literacy is not only the work of librarians, but of all faculty, the AiA project gave us the opportunity to investigate the instructional conditions that contribute to IL. We also explored the degree to which the possession of IL skills has an effect on outcomes of central importance to the institution such as GPA, retention, and graduation—whether or not students received library instruction.

Additionally, we also wanted to determine if other factors had an impact on IL beyond instruction, so we also collected data on the number of books borrowed, major, and experiences with research papers of those students who took the IL test. By collecting multiple layers of data our results told us a story that a single IL test score could not.

Selecting the AiA team

The selection of our method began with several meetings of the AiA team which was comprised of administrators and faculty from several divisions and majors—all with an interest in assessment. These team members included: the Associate Provost for Assessment, who acted as an advisor at initial meetings; the Associate Dean of the College of Liberal Arts and Science, who is an expert in quantitative methods, psychometrics and statistics; a faculty member from the Geology department who also participates in assessment activities in the College of Liberal Arts and Sciences; a faculty member from Philosophy and another from Education. This diversity of disciplines allowed us to depict how IL looks in different majors. As the librarian leading the project, I came to the initiative with statistical knowledge and some expertise in quantitative research methods, psychometric evaluation, and library research methods. Our goal in composing the AiA team was to not only represent various majors and those who valued assessment and the library, but also to allow us to gain input from stakeholders at multiple levels. This input helped us in constructing and meeting goals important to the university as a whole. The factor which contributed the most to gaining a high level of participation from faculty and administrators at our university was the offer to share data and results with department chairs and deans.

The Methods

Selecting an Instrument

During the planning stage of this study, the AiA team investigated various IL tests that were both free and fee-based. These tests included Project SAILS (Standardized Assessment of Information Literacy Skills), a validated and commercially available IL test developed at Kent State University (2015).[3] Another test considered was iSkills, a test developed by the Educational Testing Service (ETS) that assesses students on how they evaluate, create, define, synthesize and use different types of information via scenario-based problems and tasks. The costs of these two assessments prohibited their use however. Therefore, the researchers adapted the *Beile Test of Information Literacy for Educators* (B-TILED)[4] to be non-subject specific. The B-TILED is a 22 item test with 13 additional demographic and self-perception items. The test covers four of the five IL standards as articulated by ACRL's IL Standards for Higher Education[5] and was originally a part of the Project SAILS initiative. The B-TILED has been widely used in Education dissertations and has previously demonstrated reasonable reliability and validity.

In addition to the IL assessment, the questionnaire also asked students about their experiences with research papers, types of library instruction they had received, and for permission to look up other outcome data at a later date. Three hundred and three participants provided us with their student identification numbers and consent.

The Sampling Strategy

We utilized several sampling methods in order to receive the most responses to the test. First, all members of the AiA team that were in distinctly different disciplines (Geology, Psychology, Education, Physical Education and Sports Sciences, and Philosophy) administered the test to all of the students in all of their classes (two classes per faculty member). Students were offered extra credit for participation, which resulted in a 95% participation rate. While these cluster samples were not random, they did reduce the problematic bias that comes when tests are completed only by students who are inclined to answer surveys or who are generally good students. The second sampling strategy involved asking the administrators of each school at the University if they would send the survey to their faculty to be administered to entire classes (and therefore retain the previous cluster sampling strategy). The School of Health Sciences agreed, and several faculty members forwarded the test to their classes which resulted in a participation rate of about 90%. These students too received extra credit. The School of Education agreed to send the survey to all education students directly instead of through faculty/classes. Out of 1250 Education students (graduate and undergraduate) 123 completed the survey (a 10% response rate). These students were offered a chance to win a $100 gift card for their participation. In total we received 455 responses to the IL test.

How Well Did Our Method Address our Inquiry Question?

The methods we employed were intended to generalize our findings using a reasonably sized sample, as free from bias as possible. Using a previously published and validated measure was essential to meeting our goal. Often researchers try to reinvent the wheel when looking to use measures. There are many published and tested instruments readily available in the library literature, however. Additionally, it was also important to consider what other factors beyond the library might contribute to both IL competency and student success in general. Therefore we also collected data on book borrowing and research experiences. We also ensured our ability to collect additional data along the way by adding a question on the test that asked the students for their identification numbers and permission to look up additional data from our institutional research unit. By adding this question we left room to expand our study at a later date. With these methods we were able to analyze our data in multiple ways.

Limitations

The limitations of quantitative research, particularly when using a survey or test, are the inability to determine *why* students answered a question in the way that they did. Further, given that the students had no stake in the test, beyond getting extra credit for participation, it is impossible to determine whether students randomly selected answers to test questions. We tried to mitigate this problem by first eliminating responses that took students less than three minutes. Additionally, looking at the distribution of scores to see if they are on a normal curve allowed us to determine whether we should be concerned about the sample of responses we collected. Finally, although few librarians have expertise in the psychometric evaluation of a test, it is important that some type of validation analysis be conducted on a measure to ensure that it is testing what it is intended to measure.

Suggestions for Replicating our Methods

If a researcher is looking to employ quantitative methods that might produce generalizable results, it is important to understand how to construct the most appropriate, effective, and non-biased sampling strategy. Too often, because it is difficult, library research depends on convenience samples. The profession desperately needs to move away from this weakness. In the same vein, librarian-researchers using quantitative methods should also have an understanding of what confidence intervals mean and how P values relate to confidence intervals—that is, what does it really mean to be statistically significant? A librarian researcher does not need to be a statistician, but he or she should understand the basics.

Institutional research offices can often help ensure that the instrument being used is appropriate and can also help with collecting additional data. If the researchers are not well versed in statistics, it is helpful to bring in a faculty member who is. Many times data do not reveal to us what we expect or hope it will, yet there are methods by which we can employ alternative statistical tests that we may not have considered previously. Further, it is possible to recode numerical data into categories that will assist us in telling a different (if not better) story about what our results really mean. These methods can highlight what researchers should do next in their investigation. For example, when employing a treatment/control group design (often utilized when testing whether a particular teaching intervention or service is effective), most research will use a t-test or ANOVA to compare the groups on a variable. If no significant differences are found between groups, a researcher may feel that their data are useless and have no story to tell. However, by recoding the variables and flipping around the data, a regression analysis (a logistic regression in particular) can tell you what variables significantly predicted or contributed to the outcome that was determined (e.g., the score on an IL test). We employed this method of data analysis when our results proved one-dimensional and unsatisfactory. That is, library instruction did not, by itself, indicate a significant difference between students who passed the IL test and those who did not. By re-categorizing the variables and using a regression analysis we were able to determine that students who had experiences writing research papers that required library resources were far more information literate than students who only had instruction or had not written many papers. In this way we were able to lend more complexity to our inquiry than was first considered. It was integral to telling the story of "the why" of our data.

Other Methods to Address this Line of Inquiry

I am a proponent of project-based assessment. Designing a real life problem to be solved (much like the examples used in the iSkills test by ETS, mentioned above) allows the researcher to fully evaluate the extent to which a student has demonstrated IL (or other skills). By using a well-defined rubric and multiple raters who have been trained, a student's abilities can be determined on a greater level of analysis. Of course, this method is more time consuming, and it is difficult to get students to participate in this kind of study without some type of remuneration. However coupling the results of this kind of analysis with the results of a test such as the one used in this investigation, can validate (or indicate problem areas in either method) the results of the study. The more layers of data collected the better.

Conclusion

The data analysis revealed that while library instruction was not a significant predictor of information literacy competency, experiences with research papers requiring library resources and use of the library's book collection contributed significantly to information literacy skills. The results of our project indicated that instruction (whether "one-shot" or credit bearing) should be coupled within meaningful assignments requiring sustained engagement with library resources. On campuses assessment may often be met with wariness or timidity, however, conducting inquiry that will provide investigators with data with which to make improvements to instruction and policy can only benefit stakeholders and students. Lastly, it is important to consider the potential outcomes of your data. What do you do when you don't get the results you want or expect?

Notes

1. "Statement of Mission and Goals," Hofstra University, http://www.hofstra. edu/About/about_mission.html
2. Megan Oakleaf, *Value of Academic Libraries: A Comprehensive Research Review and Report* (Chicago: Association of College and Research Libraries, 2010), accessed May 1, 2015, http://www.ala.org/acrl/sites/ala.org.acrl/files/ content/issues/value/val_report.pdf
3. Kent State University, "Project SAILS (Standardized Assessment of Information Literacy Skills)," Project SAILS, https://www.projectsails.org
4. Penny M. Beile O'Neal, "Development and Validation of the Beile Test of Information Literacy for Education (B-TILED)" (doctoral dissertation, University of Central Florida, 2005), https://ezproxy.callutheran.edu/log-in?url=http://search.proquest.com/docview/305363702?accountid=9839
5. Task Force on Information Literacy Competency Standards in Higher Education, *Information literacy competency standards for higher education.* (Chicago: Association of College and Research Libraries, 2000), accessed May 1, 2015, http://www.ala.org/acrl/standards/informationliteracycompetency

CHAPTER 13

Assessing Graduating Seniors' Information Literacy Skills

Jill S. Shoemaker

Brennan Library, Lasell College
jshoemaker@lasell.edu

LASELL COLLEGE IS A small private institution located in the suburban area of Boston. A majority of the students live on campus. Majors include Fashion, Business, Communication, Human Services, Allied Health, Justice Studies, Education, Humanities, and Sport Management. Since our college is moving toward a new general education multi- disciplinary core curriculum, it was considered an optimal time to assess the graduating seniors' information literacy skills. The project's primary inquiry question was "Do we graduate students with sufficient information literacy skills to successfully enter into the workplace or graduate school?" Prior to this project, we had satisfactory data regarding our entering first year students. This was our first attempt to review the information literacy or research skills of our seniors.

Information literacy assessment can be very challenging. However, it is a "valid outcome of higher education that should be assessed in the classroom, across programs, and on an institutional level much the same way that other learning outcomes are assessed."[1]

Planning

Since I had used citation analysis as an assessment tool for two prior information literacy internal projects, I thought that this method would provide sufficient data for analysis. Upon reading the *Value of Academic Libraries*, however I was impressed by the concept of triangulation, "where multiple methods are used to find areas of convergence or data from different methods with an aim of overcoming the biases or limitations of data gathered from any one particular method."[2] Given the time constraints, I decided that in addition to citation analysis conducting small focus groups and creating a survey would be feasible. Surveys offer a broad insight into a population, while focus groups add the personal element and a wealth of qualitative and anecdotal data.

My next step in this process was to meet with faculty members who represented a variety of our academic disciplines. Our discussions were informal but touched upon a variety of themes including student learning, criteria for grading, and guidelines for number and types of source requirements. Faculty were honest and offered positive feedback as well as their concerns. Several of the academic departments are moving toward a two-semester capstone, with one semester concentrating on research and the following semester on writing.

Citation Content Analysis

Although analyzing work cited pages or bibliographies can be labor intensive, it is a wonderful method of understanding students' research logic or information-seeking habits. For scoring, I wanted to revise or create a rubric that would be discipline neutral. Since I was the only person to assess the citations, I was not concerned about norming or different scoring by other librarians.

I found a rubric that I could work with in Reinsfelder's article on citation analysis.[3] Although I maintained the original format, I changed the criteria to reflect my assessment priorities and outcomes. The five graded areas were relevance, authority/accuracy, currency, purpose, and citation. I analyzed and scored the capstone papers that had been uploaded to our MOODLE site for assessment. I reviewed 44 bibliographies representing nine majors. The papers included single-author and multiple-author works. All the data were saved to an Excel spread sheet. Excel is a useful tool to save and manipulate the data and to create graphs.

This was truly a learning experience, as I tracked each website to recreate each student's initial search strategy. Business, Hospitality and Event Management, and Criminal Justice had the lowest scores. I will periodically assess these capstone papers on a biennial basis.

Surveys

Surveys or tests can be very useful in gathering quantitative assessment data. When creating a survey, it is important to limit the number of survey questions and try to insure that the questions are easy to read and understand. In order to facilitate a meaningful survey, it is extremely important to obtain the support of administration, faculty, and students. It is useful to recruit some faculty members and students to proofread the questions for clarity. Although our Institutional Research Director was planning to be on maternity leave, she did offer to link our survey to students' email addresses and donated $100 for gift cards. The first question required students to sign a release statement prior to listing their Lasell email. Faculty members welcomed me into their classes in order to conduct the survey. This process validated my request that students take the time to answer the questions honestly. Although I explained the assessment tool as a survey, some of the students referred to it as a test. I explained that the questions were targeted to gain a better understanding of our graduating students' level of library research skills.

The survey consisted of thirteen questions. For additional clarity, my Assessment in Action (AiA) team members[4] analyzed and edited the questions. The Chair of Humanities Department suggested that we have one question related to citation from the Internet and plagiarism. I asked our history professor his opinion about adding a question regarding primary source material. Since our core curriculum has been moving toward an interdisciplinary structure, he thought that this would be a good idea. Of the remaining eleven questions, three related to scholarly articles. In addition, evaluating websites, use of Lexis-Nexis versus Google, citation, use of bibliographies, definition of the word bias, and search strategy were each the focus of one question. The remaining two questions were traditional library queries. One question asked students to describe the first two things that they would do as they began a research project. The final question asked students to identify strategies they used, including use of the library for the website, checking out books, or exploring databases.

The highest scoring method was checking out books from our library, while a request for an article through interlibrary loan was least popular. These responses appeared to be honest and mirrored student bibliographies and focus group feedback.

Respondents were 160 out of 319 graduating seniors; this was a valid sample.

Survey Monkey was used to conduct the survey. It is extremely user friendly for gathering data. Students were thrilled to be entered into a drawing for one of two $50 Visa gift cards.

Focus Groups

Prior to creating the focus groups, I asked academic administration for financial support. I was given $500 for twenty gift cards to our bookstore. This was an excellent incentive for our students. I solicited feedback from our colleagues. I met with our Chair of Humanities in order to discuss and read the feedback from an earlier Humanities focus group. I queried my colleagues at our network reference meeting, soliciting their thoughts on what would be of interest to ask students. After the initial themes were in place, I emailed several Lasell faculty members for suggestions of qualified student participants. I required a group of dependable students who represented a variety of majors. I selected three different times for sessions. Students were informed that they would receive a $25 gift card to the bookstore for participating in a one hour focus group. They signed a release, which maintained their anonymity.

I wanted to offer a very relaxed, fun, and honest session. I divided the questions into five areas of discussion: introductions, library sessions during their first year of college, individual research process, professors, and librarians/library. I audio taped each session and had a scribe to take notes.

The students were incredibly talkative and candid about their academic experiences at Lasell. Since all of the students are required to attend English 101 and English 102 library sessions during their first year at Lasell, it was interesting to note what they remembered. The most significant interaction between students involved their capstone papers. The psychology and allied health students stressed the use of scholarly research and literature reviews, while the fashion communication students were not familiar with literature reviews at all. We all laughed as we learned the differences among the majors and their resource requirements for a capstone or final project. The twenty students represented thirteen different majors. Eight of the twenty students planned to go to graduate school in the near future. When one provides a safe and confidential environment, a focus group can generate a wealth of impressive and unique qualitative data.

Limitations

This assessment project provided snapshot of our graduating seniors. I had a small window of time in which to gather and analyze the data and I was restricted by class schedules, as well as faculty and student schedules.

Since the focus groups were conducted during the month of February, unexpected weather conditions were also a real concern. Due to inclement weather, classes were canceled during our second focus group. Since the majority of students lived on campus, they all graciously agreed to stay and complete their hour commitment. The ideal assessment project would track the same group of students for four years. Such an undertaking would demand a large investment of time, staffing, and money.

Suggestions and Recommendations

There are several key ingredients to a successful assessment project: a plan based on goals and outcomes, assessment tools, feasibility, schedules, and deadlines. Although you might have assistants, the project is your responsibility from start to finish. Develop assessment tools that you feel confident will work for your purposes. Share your ideas with faculty, and ask for feedback and participation. Have realistic expectations regarding number of participants. Food and prizes are a plus for any survey or focus group. When designing a survey or test, straightforward multiple choice questions work best for Survey Monkey. Education and library literature provide many samples of useful rubrics. When constructing a rubric, focus on the criteria or outcomes and grading system. It is best to keep it very simple.

Alternative assessment projects to explore will range from one-minute surveys during a class session to detailed ethnographic studies. Research diaries or logs, worksheets, portfolios, annotated bibliographies, and individual student interviews are all creative methods of assessment. Most important for any partnership, a librarian must cultivate a sense of shared community among administration, faculty, library colleagues, and students.

Notes

1. Ralph Catts, "Some Issues in Assessing Information Literacy," in *Information literacy around the World: Advances in Programs and Research,* Christine Bruce and Philip Candy eds., (Wagga Wagga: New South Wales, Australia: Center for Information Studies, Charles Stuart University, 2000), 271–83 quoted in Elizabeth Fuseler Avery ed., *Assessing Student Learning Outcomes for Information Literacy Instruction in Academic Institutions* (Chicago: American Library Association, 2003), 8.
2. Richard P. Keeling, Andrew F. Wall, Ric Underhile and Gwendolyn J. Dungy, *Assessment Reconsidered: Institutional Effectiveness for Student Success* (International Center for Student Success and Institutional Accountability, 2008), quoted in Megan Oakleaf, *Values of Academic Libraries: A Comprehensive Research Review and Report* (Chicago: Association of College and Research Libraries, 2010), 32.
3. Thomas L. Reinsfelder, "Citation Analysis as a Tool to Measure the Impact of Individual Research Consultations," *College & Research Libraries* 73, no. 3 (May 2012): 263–277.
4. Assessment in Action Team members: Carole Center, Ph.D., Joann M. Montepare, Ph.D., Catherine Zeek, Ed.D.

Recommended Readings

Cunningham, Avril. "Using "Ready-to-Go" Assessment Tools to Create a Year Long Assessment Portfolio and Improve Instruction." *College & Undergraduate Libraries* 13, no. 2 (December 2006): 75–90.

Mackey, Thomas P. and Trudi E. Jacobson, eds. *Collaborative Information Literacy Assessments: Strategies for Evaluating Teaching and Learning.* New York: Neal-Schuman, 2010.

Mohler, Beth A. "Citation Analysis as an Assessment Tool." *Science & Technology Libraries* 25, no. 4 (June 2005): 57–64.

Radcliff, Carolyn J., Mary L. Jensen, Joseph A. Salem, Jr., Kenneth J. Burhanna and Julie A. Gedeon. *A Practical Guide to Information Literacy Assessment for Academic Librarians.* Westport, Conn: Libraries Unlimited, 2007.

Young, Virginia E. and Linda G. Ackerson. "Evaluation of Student Research Paper Bibliographies: Refining Evaluation Criteria." *Research Strategies* 13, no. 2 (Spring 1995): 80–93.

Zoellner, Kate, Sue Samson and Samantha Hines. "Continuing Assessment of Library Instruction to Undergraduates: A General Education Course Survey Research Project." *College & Research Libraries* 69, no. 4 (July 2008): 370–383.

CHAPTER 14

Using Single-Case Research Design to Assess Course-Embedded Research Consultations

John Watts

University of Nevada, Las Vegas
john.watts@unlv.edu

FOR THE ASSESSMENT IN Action (AiA) project at Webster University we sought to answer the following research question: How do required research consultations with a librarian impact student learning in a graduate-level course? To answer this question we used a single-case research design with multiple baselines across participants.[1] While single-case research design is infrequently if ever used in library assessment, it is common in the fields of clinical psychology, education, and rehabilitation. The method allows investigators to quantify changes in behaviors of individuals or small groups over time because subjects act as their own control.[2] In practice researchers study the behavior of a subject over some time to create a baseline. After a baseline is established investigators perform an intervention aimed at changing current behavior. Following the intervention investigators observe behavior in order to identify change.[3] We chose this method because of institutional context, disciplinary focus, relationship between librarian and faculty member, and the research question.

Institutional Context

Webster University is a private university with an enrollment of approximately 22,200 students located in Webster Groves, Missouri.[4] One of Webster University's core values is a "personalized approach to education through small classes and close relationships with faculty and staff."[5] One of the best practices for assessment identified by *The Value of Academic Libraries: A Comprehensive Research Review and Report*[6] is to align an assessment plan with the goals and values of your institution. To that end it seemed especially fitting that we prioritize direct student contact on the part of the librarian that emphasized a personal approach to information literacy (IL) instruction. As the liaison to the School of Education, my work focused on one-shot IL instruction and individualized research consultations for undergraduate and graduate courses in various programs within the school. Instruction statistics indicated that the majority of my instruction occurred in research-intensive graduate courses. Because we sought to assess the impact of IL instruction in areas of greatest need it made sense to target a graduate course for this assessment project.

Relationship with Faculty and Course Size

In the year prior to the assessment project I built a strong working relationship with a professor in the School of Education in order to embed required one-on-one research consultations into her research methods course situated in the Master of Special Education program. She was open to collaboration for this project and required her students to complete the work necessary to produce the observable behaviors that yield meaningful assessment data. When we launched our assessment project ten students were enrolled in the course. Although small, this size was appropriate for a single-case research design.

Research Question

Anecdotally the professor and I considered the required research consultations with the students' subject librarian (me) to be a success in the year prior to the assessment. She received fewer emails from desperate students who were struggling to find relevant information for their literature reviews and I was happy to work closely with students in order to tailor my instruction to their information needs. However even with such a small cohort there was a considerable amount of time spent on coordinating meetings, preparing for the consultations, and actually meeting with the students. Therefore it was crucial to illustrate the impact of the consultations in order to properly calculate the sustainability of this partnership. To that end we developed this research question: How do required research consultations with a librarian impact student learning in a graduate-level course?

Secondary Method: Focus Group

After choosing single-case research design as a primary method the campus team decided that a focus group would be a complementary method to the single-case design. According to the literature on mixed methods research designs, combining quantitative and qualitative elements of assessment can help to validate one form of data with another. It also can provide support if data from the single-case design did not yield the desired results.[7] The choice to use a focus group rather than a survey was based on the social nature of focus groups and their ability to allow participants to think through questions and build on each other's comments.[8] This was appropriate for a cohort of students who had an established culture of building on one another's ideas or challenging those with which they did not agree.

Single-Case Research Design in Practice

For our project a class of ten graduate students was divided into three groups, the first two consisting of three students each and the third having four. Baseline data were collected for the dependent variable, which were the student responses to weekly research scenarios developed by the professor and me and posted on the course learning management system. Each of these scenarios described a person in the midst of searching for articles on a given topic. Included with each scenario was the topic of the search and a list of the articles the hypothetical person had already discovered.

After reading the scenario students were asked to provide as many recommendations as they could to improve the search results of the student in the scenario. Additionally, students were required to provide rationales for each of their recommendations. The faculty member and I scored these recommendations and rationales using a self-designed rubric. Student scores were compared before and after each student's one-on-one research consultation with me.

Focus Group in Practice

On the final day of the research methods class students participated in a focus group. In order to encourage students to speak freely about their experiences with the research consultations we invited a faculty member from the School of Education who was not involved in the project to moderate the focus group. We used two voice recorders, one acting as a backup in the event that the primary recorder failed. Students were asked a series of eight questions addressing their experiences with the research consultations as well as several questions exploring their general experiences with research as graduate students. The session lasted a total of forty minutes. A third party subsequently transcribed the recording so that comments were anonymous. We coded comments for themes using the constant comparison method.[9]

Methods and Research Question

We set out to identify the impact of research consultations on student learning in a small cohort of students. The single-case research design is meant to pinpoint the impact of interventions on subjects without the luxury of a large sample size. Since we considered research consultations to be interventions, this method served our study well. Several students were able to provide more advanced search strategies in their responses to the weekly prompts after the research consultation and therefore scored higher on the rubric.

The focus group gave students the opportunity to reflect on the impact of the librarian on their learning with the use of more open-ended questions such as "How did personal attention in the form of the one-on-one research consultation with a librarian affect your experience in this class?" Here we were able to look more closely at how students learned more complex skills like evaluating sources for relevancy and back-chaining references from a relevant source. The focus groups also allowed us to explore other aspects of the consultation such as how students' perceptions of the librarian shifted from that of someone who only curates information to someone who possesses the skills of a teacher. This additional layer provided important insight into their experiences. Therefore the mixed methods allowed us to look directly and indirectly at the impact of the librarian on student learning.

Limitations

We encountered several limitations with the single-case research design. Though the team had established learning outcomes and a lesson plan for the research consultations, fidelity to the lesson plan wasn't always possible. Addressing the individual needs of the students was more important than rigid adherence to the plan. So some learning outcomes upon which the single-case scenarios were built could not be addressed in all research consultations. This inconsistency interfered with some students' responses to the prompts. Moreover the single case research design did not give the most comprehensive assessment of learning because each scenario focused exclusively on search strategies, which is only one of the many crucial research skills necessary for success in graduate school.

Students were required to respond to a prompt each week for eight weeks in the course site of the campus learning management system. They received participation credit for their responses and were not scored on how well they answered each prompt. This resulted in a low-stakes assignment compared to other, larger assignments throughout their semester. Therefore students might not have made their best efforts at responding to the prompts. Additionally, two students performed erratically—one scored progressively lower toward the end of the semester and another scored higher immediately after the consultation, lower in the middle of the semester, and higher again in the final two weeks. We speculated that outside factors affected their work.

Time commitment was also a limitation because the single-case design required weekly check-ins with students to remind them to complete the prompts before the deadline as well as follow up with those students who had missed deadline completely. Scoring the eighty scenarios was also time-consuming because the professor and I sought agreement on our scores. This required us to score each response individually and then meet to discuss the scenarios we scored differently and make changes to our scores accordingly. The individual scoring took four hours and we met for two hours to reach agreement.

While the focus group produced insight into student learning, it had two limitations. First, according to best practices for collecting qualitative data holding one focus group with a class does not yield the most reliable data.[10] Focus groups are typically held multiple times with different groups of participants using the same or similar questions so that investigators can see patterns. Ideally this focus group would be held with multiple classes in order to gather significant themes across responses. Second, though a third party facilitator unaffiliated with the class and the project guided the focus group and the recording was transcribed, students had built relationships with the professor and me over the semester. They knew that we would eventually examine the transcript, and even with anonymity those relationships might have persuaded them to speak more positively about their experiences with the consultations than if we were strangers.

Expertise

One of the many benefits of working with a professor from the School of Education was the expertise she brought to both single-case research design and focus groups. Having employed both methods in her own research in special education, she was able to provide guidance in the design, delivery, and reporting of our project findings. As I had no experience with either method in practice, her guidance was instrumental to the project's success.

Our third team member on this project was the Head of Institutional Effectiveness at Webster University. She was able to offer expertise regarding what tools would work best when collecting data, and how to store the data we collected. Most importantly, she advised us to use the focus group to complement the single-case design. Working with a member of University Administration also lent the project visibility on campus.

We invited a faculty member from the School of Education to conduct our focus group. This was doubly helpful. First, because she was not connected to the project students felt more comfortable speaking openly. Second, she had extensive experience conducting focus groups in her own research. Moderating a focus group can be challenging because the moderator must encourage participants to speak openly and conversationally with each other while keeping the group on track with the designated questions.[11]

Other Uses for Single-Case Research Design

This method is best employed with a single student or students in small groups. Groups could be academic or co-curricular and composed of undergraduates or graduates. For example one target audience could be a small class of undergraduate students writing a senior thesis who are required to meet individually with a librarian. Alternately, it could be students hired by the university to give tours and required to meet with a librarian before they can lead the tours on their own. In either case the small groups would need to be committed participants, which will require faculty or staff buy-in in addition to that of the students.

One additional way single-case research design could be utilized in libraries is to measure the change in skills of library student assistants after a training session. Student assistants are a rare, captive audience for librarians and a group that could be observed over a period of time. For instance, librarians who train students to work on a reference desk can implement a similar model to our design. The librarian could ask students to complete a task like a response to a scenario for several weeks. Once a baseline is set a training session would occur. After the training session the librarian continues to collect responses from students. Responses would be scored using a rubric and the scores prior to the training session would be compared against the scores post-training session.

Alternatives to Single-Case Research Design

One similar method for looking at changes in behavior before and after a research consultation is the pre- and post-test. Librarians could request that students complete a short test of information literacy skills prior to the research consultation and then complete the same test after the consultation. Scores from both tests would be compared to identify whether or not students improved. This method is more common and less time-intensive than single-case research design. However research posits that pre-and-post-tests lack validity when applied in educational settings.[12]

Since one of the limitations of single-case research design is that it provides a narrow insight into a student's information literacy skills, a more comprehensive and authentic approach to student learning outcomes assessment is to evaluate student work using an information literacy rubric tailored to the assignment.[13] Doing so would provide a more holistic understanding of students' IL skills. Also, assessing more high-stakes assignments like final papers or projects will yield more realistic and meaningful results because students are more invested in the work being assessed.

Notes

1. Alan E. Kazdin, *Single-Case Research Designs: Methods for Clinical and Applied Settings* (New York: Oxford University Press, 1982), 132.
2. Ibid., 3.
3. Alan E. Kazdin, *Behavior Modification in Applied Settings.* (Belmont, CA: Wadsworth/Thomson Learning, 2001), 75.
4. Webster University, "Fact and Figures," Webster University, accessed May 30, 2015, http://www.webster.edu/admissions/undergraduate/facts.html
5. Webster University. "Webster University Mission Statement," Webster University, accessed May 30, 2015, http://www.webster.edu/faculty/faculty_resource_guide/welcome/mission.html
6. Megan J. Oakleaf, *The Value of Academic Libraries: A Comprehensive Research Review and Report* (Chicago, IL: Association of College and Research Libraries, American Library Association, 2010), 29–32, accessed May 1, 2015, http://www.acrl.ala.org/value/?page_id=21
7. Raya Fidel, "Are We There Yet? Mixed Methods Research in Library and Information Science," *Library & Information Science Research* 30, no. 4 (2008): 266–267, doi:10.1016/j.lisr.2008.04.001.
8. Richard A. Krueger and Mary Anne Casey, *Focus Groups: A Practical Guide for Applied Research* (Thousand Oaks, CA: Sage Publications, 2015), 4–5.
9. Barney G. Glaser and Anselm L. Strauss, *The Discovery of Grounded Theory: Strategies for Qualitative Research* (Chicago, IL: Aldine Pub. Co, 1967), 101–109.
10. Krueger and Casey, *Focus Groups: A Practical Guide*, 21–22.
11. Ibid., 85.
12. Emma Marsden and Carole J. Torgerson, "Single Group, Pre- and Post-Test Research Designs: Some Methodological Concerns," *Oxford Review of Education* 38, no. 5 (October 2012): 593, doi: 10.1080/03054985.2012.731208.
13. Megan Oakleaf, "Staying on Track with Rubric Assessment: Five Institutions Investigate Information Literacy Learning," *Peer Review* 13/14, no. 4/1 (September 2011): 20–21.

CHAPTER 15

Assessing Online Graduate Students

Mary Francis

Dakota State University

mary.francis@dsu.edu

THE KARL E. MUNDT Library serves the students of Dakota State University (DSU), a small public university in Madison, South Dakota. DSU has a population of approximately 3,000 students and offers 33 baccalaureate degrees, seven master degrees, and one doctoral degree. The University has a state mandated mission to focus on technology and its integration into coursework.

DSU was selected to take part in ACRL's Assessment in Action (AiA) program in its initial round. Our goal was to evaluate the library's impact on the learning of students earning a Master of Science in Educational Technology (MSET) degree. The librarian lead was joined by two faculty members, Dr. Lynette Molstad and Dr. Don Wiken who taught classes within the program and the Director of Institutional Effectiveness and Assessment, Carrie Ahern. The MSET program is offered almost completely online, with students required to be on campus for two classes. This combination of distance education and graduate studies required a different instructional and assessment approach than the traditional in-person, undergraduate instruction that had been offered by the library for years.

The information needs of graduate students can be varied and complex. This was no different for the two courses that were a part of this assessment. Due to the needs and requirements within the two courses taught by the faculty members, different instructional approaches were undertaken. This variety of instruction methods also speaks to the idea that "offering training in a variety of formats (e.g. one-on-one consultations, one-shot classes, workshops, online learning) at different events during a graduate student's coursework can address the needs of different learners."[1]

Assessment in Action Project

Courses

The course LT 785: Research Methods in Educational Technology was focused on research methods. It was intended to prepare students to be critical consumers of research within the education field. The library instruction unit focused on the general research process. This included search techniques, locating resources, and evaluating and using the information. The second course, LT 741: Introduction to Distance Education, covered distance learning and required the students to write a position paper as well as review research articles.

Instruction Offered

Within the course LT 785, students were provided with an online tutorial composed of videos and readings. While not quite self-paced, this course allowed students to move through the material individually. The course was composed of a variety of units, with one unit opened per week within the Course Management System. The students were given a total of three weeks to complete the content. The library unit had to be completed in steps, with each section opening after the one before was completed. First, the students completed the pre-test. Second, they went through the online tutorial and completed the research process worksheet. Third, they completed a research process quiz based on their answers to the worksheet. Finally, they completed the post-test to end the unit. The librarian was given full access to the online course to view the progress of the students as well as answer any questions on the process or content.

In the course LT 741, students were instructed to individually contact a librarian to discuss the appropriateness of an article for a graduate level course. As these students were online, they were provided with an email address for a librarian to contact. They would select an article and then discuss its reliability and quality with the librarian. The librarian was able to provide individual instruction focusing on the understanding of the students.

AiA Project Topic

Within the MSET program, the students are expected to conduct research and utilize the library to achieve different outcomes. In preparing for the AiA program, one overarching topic was considered: library services for education graduate students.

Inquiry Questions and Outcomes

Due to the different expectations of the courses, the project developed two inquiry questions each with a different outcome.

- LT 785 inquiry question: How does completing an online tutorial affect the research skills of graduate students in education? Outcome: Students who complete an online tutorial will understand and successfully work within the research process.
- LT 741 inquiry question: How does interacting with a librarian affect the research skills of graduate students in education? Outcome: Students who consult with a librarian will find and use more appropriate resources for their assignments and research papers.

Assessment

LT 785 students were assessed with a pre-/post-test as well as a worksheet which had them provide answers corresponding to the steps they would take while going through the research process. Another data point for the assessment was the student's self-reported time of completion for the tutorial. LT 741 students were assessed using the grade of their final position paper written for the class. The position paper scores from the previous semester were used as a baseline for comparison.

Results

There were thirty-one students in the LT 785 course. Their average pre-test score was 76.8%. The average post-test score was 86.19%. A paired t-test showed that the difference between the pre- and post-test scores was statistically significant. Statistical tests were run looking for correlations between the other variables, but nothing of significance was found.

There were eight students within the LT 741 course. They contacted the librarian an average of three times throughout the course with the number of contacts ranging from one to seven. They averaged 90.63% on their final position paper. The year before the individual librarian instruction was established the average score on the final position paper was 88.44%. The low number of students in the classes did not allow for tests of statistical significance.

Methods

When considering which assessment method to use, a critical consideration was how the assessment would fit into the class structure. Making the assessment easy for the faculty members to implement allowed for ease of buy-in and completion of the project. It was also important that the assessment did not seem out of place to the students taking the class. An assessment that naturally developed from the work done in the class meant that the students would be able to successfully display what they had learned. This allows for a more meaningful assessment. Given the fact that the students in these classes were typically adults working full-time, the instruction methods allowed them to work at their own pace and within their own time. This meant that the assessments needed to fit into the course and student schedules as well.

The course LT 485 had an established instruction format with each week introducing a new unit so it was possible to utilize that structure as well as add an additional assessment. The library instruction offered to the course was an online tutorial that needed to be completed within a set time frame. This meant that it was a great candidate for a pre-/post-test assessment as it would look at the effect of a specific treatment.

Within the course LT 741, it was natural to look at the work that was done in the class in the form of the final position paper. This assignment required students to research a topic and integrate those finding into a paper. As the collaboration with the faculty member was developed as part of the project, it was possible to compare previous instances of the assignment in which students did not have specific, personal contact with a librarian with the papers which were written by students who did contact the librarian.

Inquiry Questions

Course LT 785. Reviewing the responses to the research process worksheet provided a good response to the inquiry question on how an online tutorial can affect the research skills of graduate students in education. The worksheet has the students show their expertise in a range of skills related to research including developing a research question, developing keywords, and the evaluation of sources. By looking at the questions which caused problems for the students, it would be possible to address those topics with additional librarian instruction. The pre- and post-tests gave a comparative method to evaluate how much the students learned by completing the tutorial and worksheet.

Course LT 741. Reviewing the final scores of the position paper offered some insight into how interacting with a librarian affects the research skills of graduate students. However, clear correlation could not be determined due to several factors impacting the assessment measure. First, the overall score on the position paper was used in the analysis. This score was also affected by other variables in addition to the sources used such as the structure and quality of writing. Secondly, there was no consideration given to the academic ability of the student in relation to the number of times he or she interacted with the librarian. A high achieving student may have had limited interactions as they understood the concepts discussed while a low achieving student may have had numerous interactions as they struggled with the process. Finally, looking solely at the position paper provided a snapshot of ability. There was no opportunity to consider whether the students' research skills developed throughout their time interacting with the librarian.

Limitations

The pre-/post-test was multiple choice. Such tests only look at the ability of students to select a correct answer rather than apply true skills and knowledge. The research process worksheet offered a more focused attempt to gather the thoughts of the students as they conduct research, but it also puts the students in an artificial situation which may not highlight their true understanding.

In looking at the final grade of the position paper, it was not possible to get a clear picture of the types of sources used by the students and their integration of research into the paper, as we were looking at one overall grade. A high grade would not necessary mean high research skills. A more effective assessment would use a rubric to look at specific criteria within the paper with at least one category related to the sources used.

Collaboration

Within this project the collaboration of course faculty was critical in implementing the assessment. The pre-/post-test questions and research process worksheet were written by the library. It was the faculty member's responsibility to get their students to complete the assignments and provide the assessment. This ownership of the assessment process is an important function of getting faculty buy-in and continual support for a program by others outside of the library. It also meant that the faculty were able to see the impact that the library instruction was having upon their students. This sharing of responsibilities also meant that the project did not require an excessive amount of time by any one individual. As assessment is just one aspect of all of team members' responsibilities, it was important that we were able to complete all of our other duties as well during the project. We were able to add the assessment of these library instructions as part of our regular routines. This allowed the project to continue into the future.

Suggestions

As noted previously, having a collaborative relationship with course faculty is critical when establishing an ongoing assessment project. They provide a connection with the students as well as offering a range of experiences. For example, the faculty in this project were able to suggest methods to sequence the library instruction and assignments offered to the students within the course management system, a process that was unknown by other members of the group.

As assessment is a process of continual development, there is much that can be done both for this specific assessment project and the overall assessment of online graduate students. While this project moves forward, it would be interesting to collect more direct evidence of student learning by analyzing particular assignments in more depth using a structured rubric. This could be a way to develop more granular details on the learning of the students. Overall, it is important for librarians to take time to assess the impact that they have on online graduate students.

Alternative Methods

As noted earlier, the assessment of LT 741 solely looking at the final grade of the position paper, did not allow for a very complete picture of the students' understanding. Specific rubrics applied to the sources used would be more effective. Another method that could be used to assess the students' understanding and ability to find quality sources would be to have them provide comments related to different evaluative criteria when they submit their articles for comments. This would provide insight into the thoughts of the students which would allow for a more focused formative assessment in the responses sent back by the librarian.

Conclusion

A joint effort of librarians and course faculty is required to ensure the development of research skills by graduate students. "While librarians are charged with imparting information literacy and information skills, it is up to the faculty teaching courses and supervising projects to ensure that students get this instruction."[2] As seen within this project, when these two groups work together, students develop these research skills and are better able to apply them in conducting their own research on topics in their field.

Notes

1. Amy Catalano, "Patterns of Graduate Students' Information Seeking Behavior: A Meta-synthesis of the Literature," *Journal of Documentation* 69, no. 2 (2013): 269.
2. Catalano, "Patterns of Information Seeking Behavior," 264.

Further Reading

Barrett, Andy. "The Information-Seeking Habits of Graduate Student Researchers in the Humanities." *The Journal of Academic Librarianship* 3, no. 4 (2005): 324–331.

Blummer, Barbara. "Providing Library Instruction to Graduate Students: A Review of the Literature." *Public Services Quarterly* 5, no. 1 (2009): 15–39.

Blummer, Barbara, Jeffrey M. Kenton and Song Liyan. "The Design and Assessment of a Proposed Library Training Unit for Education Graduate Students." *Internet Reference Services Quarterly* 15, no. 4 (2010): 227–242.

Blummer, Barbara, Sara Lohnes Watulak and Jeffrey Kenton. "The Research Experience for Education Graduate Students: A Phenomenographic Study." *Internet Reference Services Quarterly* 17, no. 3/4 (2012): 117–146.

Catalano, Amy. "Using ACRL Standards to Assess the Information Literacy of Graduate Students in an Education Program." *Evidence Based Library and Information Practice* 5, no. 4 (2010): 21–38.

Chu, Samuel Kai-Wah and Nancy Law. "Development of Information Search Expertise: Research Students' Knowledge of Source Types." *Journal of Librarianship and Information Science* 39, no. 1 (2007): 27–40.

Gibbs, David, Jennifer Boettcher, Jill Hollingsworth and Heather Slania. "Assessing the Research Needs of Graduate Students at Georgetown University." *Journal of Academic Librarianship* 38, no. 5 (2012): 268–276.

Green, Rosemary and Peter Macauley. "Doctoral Students' Engagement with Information: An American-Australian Perspective." *Portal: Libraries and the Academy* 7, no. 7 (2007): 317–332.

Hensley, Merinda Kaye and Robin Miller. "Listening from a Distance: A Survey of University of Illinois Distance Learners and Its Implications for Meaningful Instruction." *Journal of Library Administration* 50, no. 5/6 (2010): 670–683.

Ismail, Lizah. "Closing the Gap." *Reference & User Services Quarterly* 53, no. 2 (2013): 164–173.

Kayongo, Jessica and Clarence Helm. "Graduate Students and the Library: A Survey of Research Practices and Library Use at the University of Notre Dame." *Reference & User Services Quarterly* 49, no. 4 (2010): 341–349.

Rempel, Hannah Gascho, Uta Hussong-Christian and Margaret Mellinger. "Graduate Student Space and Service Needs: A Recommendation for a Cross-campus Solution." *Journal of Academic Librarianship* 37, no. 6 (2011): 480–487.

Roszkowski, Beth and Gretchen Reynolds. "Assessing, Analyzing, and Adapting: Improving a Graduate Student Instruction Program through Needs Assessment." *Behavioral & Social Sciences Librarian* 32, no. 4 (2013): 224–239.

Shaffer, Barbara A. "Graduate Student Library Research Skills: Is Online Instruction Effective?" *Journal of Library & Information Services in Distance Learning* 5, no. 1/2 (2011): 35–55.

Stitzer, Anne and Sherry Wynn Perdue. "Dissertation 101: A Research and Writing Intervention for Education Graduate Students." *Education Libraries* 34, no. 1 (2011): 4–13.

Zhang, Li, Erin M. Watson and Laura Banfield. "The Efficacy of Computer-Assisted Instruction versus Face-To-Face Instruction in Academic Libraries: A Systematic Review." *The Journal of Academic Librarianship* 33, no. 4 (2007): 479–484.

CHAPTER 16

In Their Own Words:
Evolution of Effective Search Behaviors by Medical Students and Residents at University of Connecticut Health Center

Kathleen Crea

University of Connecticut Health Center
crea@nso.uchc.edu

FACULTY, LIBRARIANS AND EDUCATIONAL administrators at the University of Connecticut (UConn) School of Medicine are interested in promoting information competencies and lifelong learning skills among graduate students. Through all phases of the medical school curriculum[1], faculty and preceptors expect students to develop proficiency in finding accurate, current medical information, and adapt their search skills to the appropriate context in which that information is needed or will be applied.

Lyman Maynard Stowe Library at UConn Health participated in the Assessment in Action (AiA) project. On the team were three librarians, an associate dean for medical education and assessment, one curriculum specialist and three physicians who are clinical faculty at UConn School of Medicine. All members agreed that the research effort should focus on demonstrating how UConn Health Library collections, library personnel and support services contribute to medical students' academic success. Having key senior faculty join the working group was important for several reasons. They are ardent supporters of Lyman Maynard Stowe Library and understand the educational value provided by access to a comprehensive bioscience library collection and responsive customer service. Over the years these faculty have worked with reference staff to create targeted library instruction for medical students, and there is an established working relationship of professional trust and educational collaboration.

Developing a Library Use Survey for Students

Team members thought that a survey of medical students would be a practical way to engage this group in order to collect current, factual data about their use of library collections, adoption of mobile medical apps and opinions about instructional services. From 1998-2003, a written Library Use Survey had been given to first- and second-year medical and dental students enrolled in Correlated Medical Problem Solving course[2] (also known as Problem Based Learning), and that research had resulted in useful feedback for faculty and librarians.

The project team met in April 2013 to create an online survey for use with all UConn medical students enrolled in Years 1 through 4, a potential population of over 400. Care was taken to craft survey questions in a manner that would encourage students to describe *in their own words* how they became effective clinical searchers during four years of undergraduate medical education. Questions were framed in a variety of formats, including open- and closed-ended questions, Likert scale, and ranking of named resources by frequency of use.

The curriculum specialist on the team created the 11-question *Library-Evidence Based Medicine (EBM)* survey using Questionmark®, an online assessment program already in use at the institution.‡ As project team leader, I was required by the institution to gain written approval from the Institutional Review Board (IRB) prior to surveying students or residents; that request was processed in a time-effective manner.

The first medical student survey request was forwarded by a senior faculty member in April 2013, and has continued each academic year since that time. Beginning in 2014, residents, post-docs and fellows at UConn Health Center have also been included in the survey population, using a slightly modified version of the questionnaire. Collecting data from two survey populations (undergraduate and graduate medical ed-

---

‡ Copies of the Library-EBM Survey can be requested from the author.

ucation groups) over time will permit comparisons of differences in how students versus residents use medical subscriptions and clinical mobile apps.

The project team discussed two other research methods before choosing to conduct an electronic survey. The first idea was to conduct pre- and post-tests with students asking about library use. This type of short survey could be done on paper easily, but data would need to be input manually to a spreadsheet program at a later date to quantify. The second idea was to conduct focus groups with students asking about use of collections and instruction, but because trained facilitators could not be found who were willing to volunteer for this activity, the idea was not pursued.

Disseminating Library-EBM Survey Data

At the end of the academic year, course directors, clinical faculty, librarians and educational administrators receive survey results from Questionmark via email. Survey data, especially voluntary comments from medical students and residents, is informative for each of these groups. Written feedback from these library users provides insight for librarian instructors on ways to improve teaching strategies for future groups and reinforces for faculty that time spent acquiring search competencies using clinical decision-support products is valued by students and new residents.

Limitations of the Methods Used

Survey participation is entirely voluntary and results are collected anonymously. No incentives or benefits are offered to those who elect to participate in this data collection. Sample sizes have been small. In 2013 and 2014[3] fewer than 15% of medical students elected to complete and return the survey. In April 2014, eighty-eight out of 600+ residents completed surveys. Broader participation by these two groups would strengthen any conclusions drawn from the data. However each survey returned offers useful statistical or anecdotal information for librarians and faculty at UConn Health to consider.

Development of Professional, Clinical and Information Competencies

Most applicants to medical school have completed 16 years or more of formal education by the time they are admitted. By gaining acceptance into a highly competitive degree program,[4] these adult learners have already demonstrated excellent scholarship skills. However, being a good scholar does not mean that they arrive with effective search skills for building clinical knowledge or synthesizing basic science information.[5] Many new medical students admit they use Google or Wikipedia as information sources for answering clinical or research questions during their first years.

Achieving information competency in medicine[6] is no small task for this group to master. The medical school curriculum at UConn is divided into pre-clinical and clinical practice years. Faculty recognize that students need instructional time with reference librarians[7] in order to gain an overview of health science information resources and effective search methods. Because course directors reserve specific blocks of time within the curriculum for small group instruction with librarians, the students get hands-on practice using a variety of library clinical sources and databases.[8] This "just in time" training during the first, second or third year introduces them to information sources that are appropriate to that particular phase in the medical school curriculum.

As their clinical knowledge base expands, their choice of sources, appraisal skills and search efficiency improves. Sequenced librarian instruction encourages the group to develop confidence in their abilities to locate medical information "on the run." Databases that may have served their educational requirements well during pre-clinical years may not be useful (or even available) for answering technical questions quickly in acute healthcare settings, when fast access to current guidelines, standard laboratory values, drug dosing, and clinical or diagnostic calculators are needed.

Clinical encounters with actual patients reinforce for students that an awareness of the context in which medical information is needed is equally important as its currency and authority. Proven information competencies gain greater significance after graduation when they become residents responsible for practicing safe, effective patient care. Putting clinical point-of-care mobile apps on their smartphones in advance of their clinical years means they have these resources literally *in hand*.

Preparing for Medical Licensure (aka Extreme Test Preparation)

In addition to completing a challenging curriculum, American medical students are required to pass a series of three national licensing examinations called the United States Medical Licensing Exam (USMLE).[9] Satisfactory scores on each step of the USMLE is a prerequisite for attaining medical licensure. Test preparation for these day-long exams represents a time-consuming but extremely motivating learning activity for these students. Ability to achieve high scores on this nationally-normed test is an important definition of "student success and achievement" for medical students (and faculty).

New residents are expected to begin medical practice having mastered six professional domains defined by the Accreditation Council for Graduate Medical Education (ACGME).[10] One of these standards includes library information competencies described in the *Practice Based Learning and Improvement (PBLI)* section.[11]

Residents who arrive for post-graduate year 1 at UConn Health may not have received EBM training with librarians at their medical schools. These groups benefit from brief library orientation sessions, and meet with library staff for assistance in loading mobile app subscriptions such as Lexicomp®, Dynamed®, Micromedex®, VisualDX® and Essential Evidence® onto their devices.

Creating a Survey? Proceed with Caution

Keep a survey brief and targeted; ask questions about only a few things. A survey that is too long, wordy or complicated won't be filled out. Give clear instructions on how to complete the survey. If questions are worded ambiguously, the answers provided will likely be as well.

Work with faculty to formulate the intent of a survey.[12] Try to find those who have experience with grant writing or who are expert at statistical analysis and invite them to join the survey team.

Once a draft of the questionnaire has been created, ask a variety of people who know nothing about the subject to complete it. Doing a pilot of the survey allows for revisions for clarity or content before distribution on a large-scale. Consider the quality of the data returned from the pilot;

was it what was expected? If not, rewrite and re-test to improve the format or wording of the questions.

Other factors to consider include:

- What group(s) will be surveyed? What do you hope to discover by surveying this group?
- How will a survey be delivered to the intended audience (e.g. a free program? Survey Monkey? Proprietary institutional software? A paper survey?)
- Which departments or personnel on campus have authority to administer a survey and control timing/method of data collection? Are librarians included in this group?
- How will the information collected by the survey be disseminated?
- Who is the audience for the survey results?
- Who owns the actual survey data after it has been collected? How will the permanency of the survey data over years be assured? Try to maintain consistency in survey content, collection methods and timing particularly if data is to be collected over years.
- Surveying a student population means results must be kept confidential. Take care to ask questions and fully understand who will be given access to the resulting data.
- Writing a one-shot survey using a paper form may bring out excellent information. Not every survey must be of epic proportions, or even administered annually.

Finally, remember that while most survey comments will likely be positive, or at least constructive; some comments may be negative (or a bit too specific). Learn from those comments to improve the content, timing or methods of instruction. Don't take criticism personally.

Final Thoughts

Conducting a library survey should be viewed as a positive marketing device for academic librarians. A survey of students represents an opportunity for librarians to *engage* these key campus constituents in order to learn more about their experiences and satisfaction using library collections, interactions with staff, quality of instruction by librarians, and use of the physical (or digital) library environment. A survey can effectively ask: "How are we doing?"

The data collected from a survey contributes to the understanding of faculty, course directors, educational administrators and provosts that library services, collections, instruction and training, and search expertise *are* indeed valuable in supporting the core values of an academic or research community. Building survey datasets over years lends authority and direction to improvements undertaken in user experiences for future groups. Survey data can support budgetary requests. Feedback from those surveyed provides insight about how effectively librarians are assisting these key campus groups in achieving intellectual, educational or vocational mastery.

Notes

1. School of Medicine, "Curriculum," University of Connecticut Heath Center, accessed June 25, 2015, http://medicine.uchc.edu/prospective/curriculum/index.html
2. School of Medicine, "Correlated Medical Problem Solving Course," University of Connecticut Heath Center, accessed June 25, 2015, http://medicine.uchc.edu/prospective/curriculum/phase1/cmps.html
3. The 2015 survey data collection and compilation was not complete at the time this was written, June 1, 2015.
4. School of Medicine, "Curriculum Goals, Objectives and Competencies," University of Connecticut Heath Center, accessed June 25, 2015, http://medicine.uchc.edu/prospective/curriculum/goals/index.html
5. Milos Jenicek, Pat Croskerry and David L. Hitchcock, "Evidence and Its Uses in Health Care and Research: The Role of Critical Thinking," *Medical Science Monitor: International Medical Journal of Experimental and Clinical Research* 17, no. 1 (January 2011): RA12-7.
6. Laure Perrier, Ann Farrell , A. Patricia Ayala, Davis Lightfoot, Tim Kenny, Ellen Aaronson, Nancy Allee, Tara Brigham, Elizabeth Connor, Teodora Constantinescu, Joanne Muellenbach, Helen-Ann Brown Epstein and Ardis Weiss, "Effects of Librarian-Provided Services in Healthcare Settings: A Systematic Review," *Journal of the American Medical Informatics Association: JAMIA* 21, no. 6 (November-December 2014): 1118–24.
7. Bryan Burford, Victoria Whittle and Gillian H. Vance, "The Relationship between Medical Student Learning Opportunities and Preparedness for Practice: A Questionnaire Study," *BMC Medical Education* 14 (October 21, 2014): 223.

8. Lyman Maynard Stowe Library, "Databases," University of Connecticut Heath Center, accessed June 25, 2015, http://libdatabase.uchc.edu/databases/databases.asp

9. United States Medical Licensing Exam (USMLE), "About the USMLE," Federation of State Medical Boards (FSMB) and National Board of Medical Examiners® (NBME®), accessed June 25, 2015, http://www.usmle.org/

10. American Council for Graduate Medical Education (ACGME), "About ACGME," American Council for Graduate Medical Education, accessed June 25, 2015, http://www.acgme.org/acgmeweb/tabid/116/About.aspx

11. School of Medicine, Graduate Medical Education, "ACGME Competencies," University of Connecticut Health Center, accessed June 19, 2015 http://gme.uchc.edu/programs/competencies.html

12. Florida Center for Instructional Technology, "Classroom Assessment, Attitude Surveys," University of South Florida, accessed June 19, 2015, http://fcit.usf.edu/assessment/attitude/surveyb.html

Further Reading

Boruff, Jill and Koren Hyogene Kwag. "Mobile Devices in Medicine: A Survey of How Medical Students, Residents, and Faculty Use Smartphones and Other Mobile Devices to Find Information." *Journal of the Medical Library Association* 102, no. 1 (January 2014): 23–30. Accessed June 21, 2015. http://www.ncbi.nlm.nih.gov/pmc/articles/PMC3878932/pdf/mlab-102-01-22.pdf

Bradley, Doreen, Gurpreet Rana, Monia Lypson, Stanley Hamstra. "A Centralized Practice-Based Learning and Improvement Curriculum for Residents and Fellows: A Collaboration of Health Sciences Librarians and Graduate Medical Education Administration." *Journal of the Medical Library Association* 98, no. 2 (April 2010): 175–178. Accessed June 21, 2015. http://www.ncbi.nlm.nih.gov/pmc/articles/PMC2859263/pdf/mlab-98-02-175.pdf

Ellaway, Rachel, Patricia Fink, Lisa Graves and Alanna Campbell. "Left to Their Own Devices: Medical Learners' Use of Mobile Technologies." *Medical Teacher* 36, no. 2 (February 2014): 130–138. Accessed June 21, 2015. http://informahealthcare.com/doi/pdfplus/10.3109/0142159X.2013.849800

Friederichs, Hendrik, Bernhard Marschall and Anne Weissenstein. "Practicing Evidence Based Medicine at the Bedside: A Randomized Controlled Pilot Study in Undergraduate Medical Students Assessing the Practicality of Tables, Smartphones, and Computers in Clinical Life." *BMC Medical Informatics & Decision Making* 14, no. 12 (December 2014): 113–117. Accessed

June 21, 2015. http://www.biomedcentral.com/content/pdf/s12911-014-0113-7.pdf

Ilic, Dragon and Kristian Forbes. "Undergraduate Medical Student Perceptions and Use of Evidence Based Medicine: A Qualitative Study." *BMC Medical Education* 10 (August 2010): 58–64. Accessed June 21, 2015. http://www.biomedcentral.com/1472-6920/10/58

CHAPTER 17

Finding the Cocked Hat:
Triangulating Assessment for Information Literacy as a College-Wide Core Competency

Brandy Whitlock

Anne Arundel Community College
bmwhitlock@aacc.edu

ANNE ARUNDEL COMMUNITY COLLEGE (AACC) established and recently revised a set of college-wide core competencies, which includes information literacy, and created a curriculum map to identify when each degree-bearing program should develop and assess these competencies. However, college stakeholders did not know to what extent our graduating students could demonstrate these competencies, nor how program curricula might be revised to improve student proficiency. The question that the Assessment in Action (AiA) team at AACC has been studying is: are there sufficient mechanisms in place at AACC that lead students to develop appropriate information literacy skills by the time they graduate?

To establish the overall assessment process of the college's core competencies, AACC's Office of Learning Outcomes Assessment (LOA) produced a Learning Outcomes Assessment Plan, in which each of AACC's ten college-wide core competencies is assessed during a two-year process. To assess a core competency, the LOA Subcommittee of the college's Committee on Teaching Learning takes a fall semester to investigate and decide on an assessment process for that specific competency. In the subsequent spring semester, the process is implemented and tested, providing an opportunity to revise the process and tool(s). After the testing phase, the process is run for the subsequent fall and spring semesters.

The timing of the first cohort of The Association of College and Research Libraries' Assessment in Action project coincided with the point in AACC's LOA Plan that information literacy was scheduled for assessment. When the process of assessing information literacy began, the assessment of another college-wide core competency, communication, had already been designed and tested. The second year of assessing communication would overlap with the first year of assessing information literacy. For communication, the LOA Subcommittee opted for an authentic assessment of graduating students' work, after discussing many possible assessment designs. Due to the need to intrude as little as possible on students' and instructors' time, and because it is extraordinarily difficult to get a representative, reliable sample from among student volunteers, the subcommittee decided against a design that would involve testing or observation external to students' normal coursework.

Because causality is extremely difficult to prove, the LOA Subcommittee focused on providing a snapshot of our graduating students' skills, rather than designing an assessment that attempted to gauge how much students learned through their AACC program curricula (e.g., pre-test/post-test). The LOA Subcommittee also considered the overall purpose of the assessment process, which is to produce information that will help stakeholders better understand the extent to which AACC graduates students are able to demonstrate appropriate competencies in these core areas, regardless of students' learning and experiences that occurred before or outside of the completion of their AACC curricula.

The LOA Subcommittee reviewed a number of possible scoring rubrics and, after much discussion, chose to develop a rubric specific to AACC's definition and conceptualization of communication as a core competency. The LOA Subcommittee felt strongly that AACC's rubric should exhibit a clear division between proficient work and non-proficient work, so a four-point scale was employed. A student artifact would be scored in each category of the communication rubric (content, organization, style/expression, and mechanics) as exhibiting exemplary, proficient, developing, or emerging communication skills. Faculty members in AACC's English and Communications department provided additional review of the resulting rubric.

AACC's Office of LOA then initiated the process of procuring student artifacts for scoring. First, the Office of LOA contacted department chairs to inform them of the process. Then, the Office of LOA, in conjunction with the Registrar's Office, developed a list of students who had applied for graduation with an associate degree. These students received an email that notified them of the upcoming assessments and provided instructions for opting out. A random sample of the graduating students was produced, between thirty and forty percent for each of the three semesters that the assessment process was deployed. The Office of LOA then visited each student's schedule of classes, looking for courses associated with communication in AACC's curriculum map.

Once a course mapped to communication was identified in a student's schedule, the Office of LOA contacted the faculty member teaching that section and asked for a sample of the student's work that demonstrated communication skills. If a faculty member could not provide a sample, the student's schedule was revisited, and the instructor of the next course mapped to communication would be contacted. Faculty members were asked to send in their assignment sheets, in addition to student communication artifacts, so that scoring could take assignment parameters into account. Once received by the Office of LOA, each sample and assignment sheet was stripped of student, course, and instructor identifiers. Then, at the college's annual Summer Institute, faculty and staff volunteers from across the college scored student artifacts, double-scoring a substantial portion, using the communication scoring rubric developed by the LOA Subcommittee.

The rubric for scoring information literacy skills was also designed by the LOA Subcommittee after consulting a number of other institutions' rubrics. The information literacy rubric covered four criteria—choice of sources, evaluation of sources, incorporation, and ethical use—along the same four-point scale outlined above. Library faculty at AACC reviewed the rubric and offered revisions. Because information literacy skills may be expressed differently within different disciplines, only library faculty were asked to score the student work gathered for this competency. All AACC librarians staff our reference desk, in addition to conducting instructional sessions for classes in most every discipline, and can draw on more college-wide context than other faculty when considering how information literacy skills are developed through curricula and how they manifest in student work.

In practice, librarians regularly scored student artifacts in only three of the four areas: choice of sources (student chooses appropriate sources; content of information), incorporation (student uses information to accomplish a specific purpose), and ethical use (student complies with institutional policies related to access and use of information, demonstrating an understanding of academic integrity). Most submissions could not be scored for the fourth category, evaluation of sources (student critically assesses sources and content of information), because most artifacts did not include evidence of how and where students searched for information, nor how they evaluated what they found.. Student research papers rarely provide such insight.

In an effort to better understand how instructors encourage students to demonstrate information literacy skills, librarians consulted the assignment sheets accompanying student artifacts. Using a checklist, librarians recorded whether assignment sheets contained instructions and expectations about the proper incorporation of appropriate informational resources. To better understand the library's role in curriculum development and deployment, the AiA team, in conjunction with library faculty members, created a survey that was administered to those instructors who sent in student artifacts. Along with the assignment checklist, the faculty survey also provides insight into how faculty members teach and assess information literacy skills.

Student artifacts allow us to assess some relevant information literacy skills among graduating students, but by utilizing the college's curriculum map, an assignment checklist, and a faculty survey, the assessment design employed by AACC's AiA team will result in a better understanding of when and how students' information literacy skills are developed and assessed. From program to assignment design, AACC's AiA project incorporates multiple perspectives that produce a better overall picture of how and to what extend our students graduate with the ability to demonstrate appropriate information literacy skills.

AACC's AiA team encountered a number of challenges in implementing its assessment methodology. It was often difficult to procure student artifacts, threatening our ability to extrapolate reliable conclusions from our sample. For the first round of information literacy scoring, the Office of LOA received a very low number of samples. So artifacts that had been submitted for communication scoring that also provided evidence of information literacy skills were identified and included among the artifacts scored for information literacy. Though the AiA team would have preferred wider deployment of the faculty survey, AACC's Office for Institutional Assessment, which oversees survey administration at the college, had concerns about sending out the AiA team's faculty survey college-wide because of the number of other surveys that faculty members were asked to complete. Though AACC's five librarians have been extraordinarily generous in volunteering to score student artifacts, the workload has proved especially burdensome because we have so few scorers. Additionally, a small pool of scorers always produces concerns about inter-rater reliability.

To steer an assessment project of this size and scope, it's helpful to have a very small, dedicated AiA team. This team can address issues with the assessment process and make decisions quickly while maintaining a bird's-eye view of—and a sustained and intense focus on—the project's overall purpose. For anyone attempting this kind of complicated methodology, it's necessary to develop and maintain excellent working relationships across campus and among librarians. Consulting and collaborating with many stakeholders at the college, AACC's AiA team works most closely with the LOA Subcommittee. The subcommittee's charter mandates faculty representation from disciplines across the college. The subcommittee also helps create, revise, and formally approve the processes and tools used for assessing college-wide core competencies. Other consultants and collaborators include AACC's Office of LOA, which facilitates scoring sessions and data collection, compilation, and reporting, as well as the AACC's Faculty Assessment Fellows, who work in their departments to spearhead and share results of assessment efforts. Our library administration and faculty have proven invaluable to the process, volunteering to help develop and then employ the assessment tools used to measure information literacy skills.

Though all of AACC's information literacy assessment tools were developed in-house, standardized assessment tools, such as knowledge and performance-based tests, may work at traditional four-year schools, where students are often residential, of traditional college age and preparation, and generally follow prescribed paths through curricula of degree-bearing programs. For many open-access schools like AACC, though, these kinds of assessment designs are simply not feasible. Perhaps most importantly, these assessment tools are rarely as valid as authentic measures of student learning. Even if they are feasible and provide excellent snapshots of student ability, standardized assessment tools can rarely provide relevant information about when and how students are supposed to develop the knowledge and skills being tested. Triangulating information from multiple perspectives—using a curriculum map, surveying faculty, and assessing the assignments students are given alongside the work students produce—provides a richer picture of when, how, and to what extent students' information literacy skills are developed in the curricula they experience.

Further Reading

Dubicki, Eleonora. "Faculty Perceptions of Students' Information Literacy Skills Competencies." *Journal of Information Literacy* 7, no. 2 (December 2013): 97–125. doi: 10.11645/7.2.1852.

Farrell, Robert and William Badke. "Situating Information Literacy in the Disciplines." *Reference Services Review* 43, no. 2 (April 2015): 319–340. doi: 10.1108/RSR-11-2014-0052.

Holliday, Wendy, Betty Dance, Erin Davis, Britt Fagerheim, Anne Hedrich, Kacy Lundstrom, and Pamela Martin. "An Information Literacy Snapshot: Authentic Assessment across the Curriculum." *College & Research Libraries* 76, no. 2 (March 2015): 170–187. doi: 10.5860/crl.76.2.170.

Oakleaf, Megan. "Writing Information Literacy Assessment Plans: A Guide to Best Practice." *Communications in Information Literacy* 3, no. 2 (2009): 80–89. http://www.comminfolit.org/index.php?journal=cil&page=article&op=view&path%5B%5D=Vol3-2009PER2&path%5B%5D=98

Rinto, Erin E. "Developing and Applying an Information Literacy Rubric to Student Annotated Bibliographies." *Evidence Based Library & Information Practice* 8, no. 3 (July 2013): 5–18. http://ejournals.library.ualberta.ca/index.php/EBLIP/article/view/19158/15725

Thonney, Teresa and Joe C. Montgomery. "The Relationship between Cumulative Credits and Student Learning Outcomes: A Cross-Sectional Assessment of Information Literacy and Communication Skills." *Journal of the Scholarship of Teaching and Learning* 15, no. 1 (February 1, 2015): 70–87. doi: 10.14434/josotl.v15i1.12954.

Warner, Dorothy Anne. *A Disciplinary Blueprint for the Assessment of Information Literacy.* Westport, CT: Libraries Unlimited, 2008.

Whitlock, Brandy and Julie Nanavati. "A Systematic Approach to Performative and Authentic Assessment." *Reference Services Review* 41, no. 1 (February 2013): 32–48. doi: 10.1108/00907321311300866.

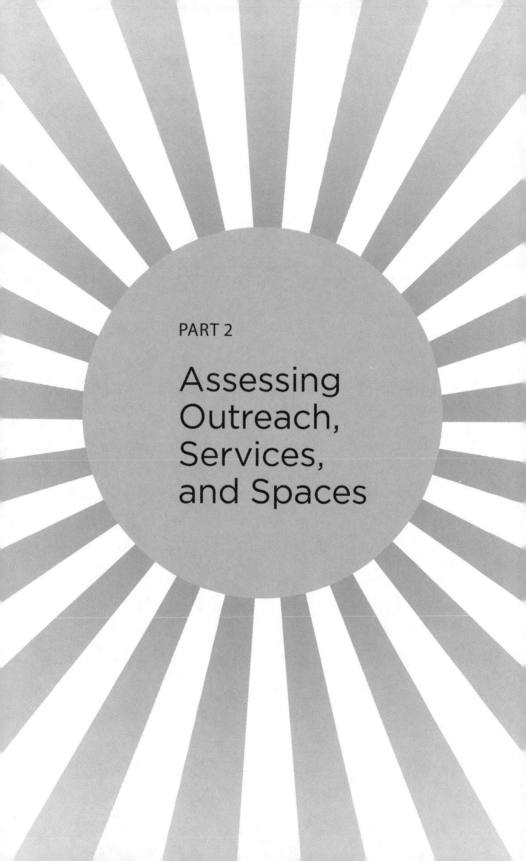

PART 2

Assessing
Outreach,
Services,
and Spaces

CHAPTER 18

Get By with a Little Help from Your Friends:

Working with Student Affairs to Engage and Assess College Students

Theresa McDevitt

Indiana University of Pennsylvania Libraries
mcdevitt@iup.edu

TRANSFORMATIONS IN COMMUNICATION AND informa-tion access/storage that accompanied the technological developments of the late 20th and early 21st -century have greatly impacted the design and function of academic libraries. Prior to this period, libraries enjoyed a rel-atively stable existence as repositories of paper and other tangible informa-tion resources. For decades they were characterized by simple, quiet, and not always comfortable study spaces, and classically trained librarians who maintained their distance, answering questions when approached from a central reference desk, and enforcing silence and borrowing policies. There was little equipment to support learning, information sharing, and project development with the exception of the odd typewriter or copy machine. Changing communication technologies have thrust the 21st -century aca-demic library into a dynamic environment where paper and other tangi-ble information resources are being digitized, discarded, or sent to off-site storage to make room for computers and comfortable seating, coffee bars, and flexible community spaces. Employees have come out from behind the reference desks (which have often disappeared) and now offer assistance in use of the technology, as well as information, necessary to assist clients to complete the more complex projects that come with the new teaching and learning environments.

This dynamic environment makes it crucial that libraries understand users' needs and desires and develop, design, or acquire spaces, resources, and services to provide for them. Informing users of all that libraries have and how, and even why, it is important to use them, is also of central importance. How do libraries connect with their clients to keep up with their swiftly changing and more diverse needs and desires? How do they inform users who can access information resources without coming into library buildings or visiting library webpages what libraries have to offer? How do libraries prove their value in the new academic environment where demonstrating impact is required of all? The answer to these new challenges lies at least partially in the development of skills in assessment and engagement of students, academic libraries largest and most dynamic clientele.

Unfortunately, the necessity of carrying out formal assessment and intentionally designing activities for the engagement of clients is relatively new to academic librarians whose training long tended to focus on developing skills related to classifying, storing, and retrieving information. Acquiring the skills necessary to do these new activities however, is not something libraries have to do alone. By looking outside of their walls, but still on their campus, they will find colleagues with extensive experience in both these areas who are only too willing to help in their Division of Student Affairs.

Our Action Project

Our Assessment in Action (AiA) project began with a problem. Indiana University of Pennsylvania (IUP) students were lacking in information literacy skills and a basic knowledge of what the library had to offer them. This was a barrier to their utilizing the IUP Libraries' spaces, services, and resources as much as they might and possibly limiting their academic success. Our idea was to draw upon the collective expertise of IUP Libraries and our Office of Housing Resident Life and Dining (OHRLD) to promote and improve information literacy skills among students in IUP's residential communities. This would be done by developing and delivering programs and services to living-learning communities related to student information literacy and academic success. The process of determining what sorts of programs and services we might develop and deploy would be grounded in, and responsive to, ongoing assessment activity.

Methods

We used a mixed method of assessment, but primarily collected qualitative rather than quantitative data. We used individually administered paper surveys and data collected with focus groups with guided questions. Our paper surveys included primarily questions containing Likert scales and a few open-ended questions to give us the opportunity to understand what students were thinking as well as learn from their creative ideas. We analyzed the data by using Excel and NVivo software.

Our inquiry question initially was "How can we draw upon the collective expertise of IUP Libraries and Office of Housing Residential Life and Dining (OHRLD) to promote and improve information literacy skills among students in IUP's residential communities?" It shifted in the course of the grant period to a more general question of "How can IUP Libraries and Division of Student Affairs collaborate to increase student library usage or to support student learning and success?" This shift resulted from student feedback that students were not likely to attend formal instructional information literacy skill development programs offered in the residence halls. Instead we found that they were more likely to participate in information library/information literacy educational games designed to create experiential learning opportunities and increase the likelihood that students would turn to the library at their point of need and were embedded into our Student Affairs Division's ongoing calendar of student engagement events. Also, we realized that without the ability to examine artifacts of learning, we would have a difficult time measuring information literacy skill development.

We divided our project into three periods: Conceptualization; Phase One; and Phase Two. Spring through fall of the first year was the conceptualization stage. Members of the team met bi-weekly to gather and analyze existing data and discuss the activities that would be carried out and how we could measure their impact. When we had a clear enough idea of our project, we worked on the development of the IRB application.

An important step involved a review of the existing library literature. We reviewed the background literature in the areas of library outreach, active and innovative methods of student orientation and educational programming. We also examined the literature which treated partnerships between academic libraries and personnel from Student Affair's Divisions to find successful examples that we might learn from. Some of the literature we reviewed can be found in the bibliography at the end of the chapter.

We applied for IRB approval and were given approval for the project. The key activity during this period was a simple first-year student library scavenger hunt. It was designed to provide students with a positive experience interacting with people in the library who could help them and a basic knowledge the location of the service desks and what services each offered. We also provided step-by-step directions on how to find a book in the catalog and on the shelves, and how to email the full-text of a journal article to themselves. The activity was educationally based, but we also wanted to make it fun for them, so we included using their cell phones and competing or entering a drawing for prizes at the end.

During the summer, the game was piloted with summer orientation groups, including upper level high school students in the Upward Bound program and beginning first-year students in a summer scholars program. Each group was divided into teams, and the first team to complete the activity was awarded library t-shirts, and all were entered into a drawing for an iPad mini that would be given away in the fall. As part of our design, each activity or program included a culminating paper survey which collected responses related to whether students enjoyed the activity, felt that they learned something useful from it, if participation impacted their likelihood of visiting the library in the future, and any comments or suggestions for improvement that they would like to offer.

Analysis of the feedback gathered in the summer session led us to revise the survey slightly, but also convinced us that students enjoyed the game and felt they learned something useful through the activity. In the fall the scavenger hunt was included as an activity during Welcome Weekend, a first-year experience orientation that takes place the weekend before classes begin. Each student who completed the scavenger hunt that weekend got a t-shirt as long as supplies lasted. They were also entered into a drawing for an iPad mini. During Welcome Weekend, only 30 students completed the activity. In hopes that we might get more students completing the activity, particularly student groups from the residence halls, we expanded the deadline to complete the activity and qualify to enter the drawing to the end of September. We advertised on social media and digital signage. A professor in Nutrition heard about the activity and included it as an assignment for her class. As a result, by the end of September around 150 students took part in the library scavenger hunt.

Later in the fall we developed a library bingo game that students could play to enter monthly drawings for library giveaways and a pizza party. This too was adopted by a professor as an assignment. Students who completed the game were asked to fill out surveys to enter the drawing. Survey results indicated students enjoyed the games, felt they learned something they would use in the future, and that playing it made it more likely that they would visit the library in the future.

Building up on our positive experience, in the spring of 2014, Phase Two, we expanded our project to develop a broader IUP Libraries frequent visitor rewards program. It was called the Library VIP Program. It was intended to increase visits to the library and attendance at library related programs. It recorded attendance with Library VIP cards and stickers. During National Library Week, students who participated in the program were included by completing a survey related to library use. All participants were entered into drawings to win a variety of donated prizes based upon the frequency of their visits. Also, students who earned 10 stickers in the contest were automatically awarded Library Success t-shirts.

Students qualified for stickers by attending a wide variety of programs. These included participating in Library focus groups (Library Student Advisory Group, the Residence Hall Association and other student groups), and attending film screenings in the library. Attendance at more general lectures which related to doing research or information literacy topics, library instruction sessions and competing in Student Success Trivia Contests were also included. A more complete list of events included can be found at: http://libraryguides.lib.iup.edu/vip

Limitations of Method

Our method was limiting in terms of how much data we could collect because of the use of paper surveys. The paper surveys were time-consuming to administer and to analyze and sometimes a student's handwriting was not legible. At many points we felt that people who had completed the activity may have failed to complete the survey for one reason or another, particularly when they did the survey for a class and the professor collected the completed games. Also, questions we asked relied on self-reported, and therefore indirect data, so this was a drawback. Additionally, we did such small scale sampling that though we had results, and valuable qualitative data, results were not in sufficient numbers to be really significant.

Outside Assistance

Many colleagues outside the library were willing to assist us in the project. The Assistant Director for Assessment and Academic Initiatives, OHRLD, and the Assistant Dean for Information & Communications Technology, IUP College of Education and Educational Technology, the Assistant Director for Student Life/ Student Leadership and New Student Success, the Center for Student Life, and the Executive Director, OHRLD were all members of the AiA project team and contributed significantly.

The Assistant Director for Assessment and Academic Initiatives, a recognized campus expert on campus in assessment, provided assistance in developing our surveys and the IRB application. The College of Education Assistant Dean, an expert on the use of NVivo, provided training in the use of this software which supported our mixed methods research. The Assistant Director for Student Life/ Student Leadership and New Student Success informed us of opportunities for embedding library activities in their schedule of engagement events and provided invaluable advice on developing the kinds of activities and games that appeal to students.

Other employees from the OHRLD and the Center for Student Life assisted by allowing us to provide library educational activities as part of required peer mentor training and helping us connect with students in Greek and other student associations about developing library-centered educational activities and using the library as a venue for educational activities. Student collaborators included members of the Residence Housing Association, graduate students in Student Affairs in Higher Education, Academic Success Mentors, and Greek society educational officers, to mention only a few. We found them all to be eager for collaboration, in sympathy with our mission of designing and carrying out engaging educational opportunities related to the library and assessment that will form the basis of improvements to these opportunities.

Advice to Others

Our project was simple and inexpensive, and could be replicated easily at other institutions of all sizes and types. The scavenger hunt orientation, piloted with summer orientation groups, offered as a general orientation activity as part of a more general orientation experience, and then offered to faculty as a do-it-yourself orientation activity to be used in their classes, was a success. Students reported that they felt they learned something and they were more likely to return to use the library later as a result of playing it. It was fairly inexpensive and demanded little staff time. It was more successful because of the advice and assistance we received from Student Affairs personnel in developing the activity in an engaging way, finding groups to pilot it with, and then embedding it in ongoing orientation activities. We would advise reaching out to Student Affairs Divisions, whose philosophy is to seek partnerships to do their work of creating the best environment for student success. It worked well for us particularly because of a very strong commitment to collaboration with outside partners in our Student Affairs Division, because we were able to agree upon a shared mission of supporting student success and our libraries could be flexible enough to accept any opportunities and advice offered.

Benefits

Working with the Division of Student Affairs has improved our understanding of what students find engaging and has also offered us increased opportunities for embedding library activities in existing student engagement calendar of events. This has led to an increase in participation in library outreach activities and increased awareness of the good things going on in the library and how it can help students. It has led to a healthy exchange of information and best practices between the Libraries and Student Affairs staff. This has been of benefit to both and has strengthened the ability of the library to serve as a central place where students turn to for information or referral, and increased not only its perceived, but its actual value to the university.

Recommendations for Change

The use of paper surveys provided some good data, but was time consuming and limiting. We feel that electronic collection and analysis of data using Qualtrics or other electronic survey tool would allow for a wider scale data collection and ease analysis of data. We also would advise using NVivo for analysis of qualitative data. A poster summarizing the project and its results can be accessed at http://libraryguides.lib.iup.edu/ld.php?-content_id=11507644.

Further Reading

Appleton, Leo and Paul Abernethy. "We Said…We Did!: A Partnership Approach to Developing Library and Student Support Services." *New Review of Academic Librarianship* 19, no. 2 (2013): 208–220.

Cahoy, Ellysa S. and Rebecca M. Bichel. "A Luau in the Library? A New Model of Library Orientation."*College & Undergraduate Libraries* 11, no. 1 (2004): 49–60.

Carter, Toni. "Reaching Your Millennials: A Fresh Look at Freshman Orientation." *Tennessee Libraries* 57, no. 2 (2007). Accessed May 29, 2015. http://www.tnla.org/?124

Crowe, Kathryn M. "Student Affairs Connection: Promoting the Library through Co-curricular Activities." *Collaborative Librarianship* 2, no. 3 (2010): 154–158.Cummings, Lara U. "Bursting Out of the Box: Outreach to the Millennial Generation through Student Services Programs." *Reference Services Review* 35, no. 2 (2007): 285–295.

Fortson, Melissa, Josh Sahib, and Brett Spencer. "Step Right Up to the Library! The Week of Welcome Carnival at the University of Alabama Libraries." *College & Research Libraries News* 72, no. 6 (2011): 350–352.

Hinchliffe, Lisa J. and Melissa A. Wong, eds. *Environments for Student Growth and Development: Libraries and Student Affairs in Collaboration.* Chicago: Association of College and Research Libraries, 2012.

Riehle, Catherine F. and Michael C. Witt. "Librarians in the Hall: Instructional Outreach in Campus Residences." *College & Undergraduate Libraries* 16, no. 2–3 (2009): 107–121.

Strothmann, Molly and Karen Antell. "The Live-In Librarian." *Reference & User Services Quarterly* 50, no. 1 (2010): 48–58.

Swartz, Pauline S., Brian A. Carlisle, and E. Chisato Uyeki. "Libraries and Student Affairs: Partners for Student Success." *Reference Services Review* 35, no. 1 (2007): 109–122.

Zitron, Liz and Courtney Drew. "Get a Clue: Partnering with Student Affairs on Student-Centered Outreach." *College & Research Libraries News* 72, no. 11 (2011): 636–641.

CHAPTER 19

ARC to Success:
Linking the "Commons" Model
to Academic Success at Central
Washington University

Courtney Paddick

Bucknell University
courtney.paddick@bucknell.edu

IN MAY 2012, THE Brooks Library, University Tutoring Services, and Career Services, received funding from the Provost to repurpose the reference area in the library to create a new "one-stop shop" for student success at Central Washington University. What emerged from this project was the Academic & Research Commons (ARC), which officially opened its doors in November 2012. The ARC brought together Reference Librarians, tutors, a career counselor, Career Services peer advisors, and new technology together in one space that focuses on collaboration and student success. Due to the quick turn-around of the project, from conception to implementation, there was little time to consider what we hoped to accomplish by bringing all three services together in one space that included collaborative technology. When I learned about Assessment in Action (AiA) I saw an opportunity to examine how the ARC contributed to student success.

The first step in the process was to identify partners for the study. Since I was looking at assessing the impact of the ARC, it made sense to bring the head of tutoring services, Prairie Brown, on to the team. Based upon a number of criteria that Prairie and I developed, we identified English

101 Composition I: Critical Reading and Responding as the best fit for the needs of the study. We identified our third partner as Dr. Loretta Gray from the English Department. Dr. Gray oversees the Teaching Assistants in the English Department that teach many of the English 101 classes.

English 101 was chosen for a number of reasons. Most students are required to take English 101 and most students take it during their first year. Since this was the first fall that the ARC was fully operational, most of these students would be unfamiliar with the space. Since English 101 is often the first introduction to college-level writing and research, it appeared to be a natural place to introduce the ARC to students. Additionally, English 101 is taught from a standard syllabus so it eliminated some of the variables in course design that another class may have provided. Over the years the Library's and Writing Center's involvement in English 101 had been sporadic. So to identify a control set of classes would not be taking away services or information they normally would have received.

Our assessment project had two objectives. First, to see if exposure to the ARC over the course of a quarter would have an impact on student success. Second, to see if this exposure to the ARC in a class would lead to repeat usage of its space and services. When developing our study we decided the best method to use would be a mix of qualitative and quantitative data. For the quantitative portion of our study, we decided to collect final course grades and final paper grades. In regards to the qualitative data, we developed a pre- and post-self-assessment to be administered to the students at the beginning and the end of the course.

The pre- self-assessment set a baseline for our study. Students were asked about their familiarity with the ARC, to assess their skill and comfort with academic writing and research, as well as whether they had ever met with a librarian or tutor for help with an assignment. The post- self-assessment asked the same information but also included several open ended questions such as: if a student had met with either a tutor and/or a librarian how was their experience and what were their major takeaways from English 101?

The other important consideration when designing our project was to have a control and test groups. In the past the Library and Writing Center's involvement in English 101 has been sporadic at best. Because of this past history, we knew that having a control group would not be eliminating services the students traditionally received. We decided upon a control group made up of three classes and a test group of three classes. For the test group, we ultimately decided that students would receive a library instruction session, a tutor-led peer editing session, and then the students would be required to meet with either a writing tutor or librarian for a one-on-one session. The library instruction session was designed to give students an overview of the ARC and to include demonstration and active learning that provided students an introduction to keyword searching in the library catalog and databases and evaluating sources utilizing the CRAAP test (Currency, Relevance, Authority, Accuracy, and Purpose). Due to some technology constraints at the time, the library sessions were held in the library computer lab rather than the ARC, but the tutor-led peer editing session took place within the ARC and the meeting with the librarian and/or tutor required the student to visit the ARC on their own time. Through this project design, students were provided an introduction to the ARC formally within their class but were also be required to visit it again on their own.

Throughout our project one of the major considerations was to find ways of assessing the impact the ARC has on student success when integrated into English 101 without being too intrusive to the class. This was the first time the ARC and the Library in general had requested this level of integration into a class and we wanted to be sure that our expectations were in line with the time that would be allocated to us. We tried to be as accommodating as possible to the needs of the English 101 instructors. This actually meant that instead of having an even number of classes in the control and test groups, we ended up with two control and four test classes.

Our method evolved as we progressed in the quarter. We realized that tracking students into the *following* quarter would provide us with a better understanding of the impact of our study. Since the Writing Center tracks all students that complete a tutoring session, we were able to see if students who met with a tutor as part of our study were more or less apt to utilize the Writing Center the following quarter. We also decided to examine the grades for students who completed English 101 as part of our study and who went on to enroll in English 102 the subsequent quarter. By tracking student grades and student meetings with a tutor during the following quarter, we were able to see if there was any residual impact from one quarter to the next.

There were several issues that we discovered with our study along the way. The decision to choose English 101 classes to work with also proved to be one of our biggest challenges. Since teaching assistants teach a number of the classes in the department, English 101 is taught using a set syllabus. What we didn't know going into the quarter was that the English 101 classes taught by teaching assistants do not meet during the final week of classes. Since the last week was when we intended to have students fill out the post- self-assessments, we had a bit of a scramble to find an alternative way to disseminate the post- self-assessments to students. We ultimately decided to add the self-assessment to Blackboard Course Management System but this significantly impacted the number of completed post self-assessments we received.

Additional communication issues resulted in the mysterious disappearance of one set of pre- self-assessments from our test group. This meant that at the end of the study we were down to three classes in our test group and two classes in our control group.

An issue that we did not anticipate going into the study was the impact of teaching assistants as graders. An English lecturer taught two of our test classes, while the four other sections of English 101 were taught by teaching assistants. The students in the classes taught by the English lecturer did significantly better than the students in the classes taught by teaching assistants. It is unclear if this was due to different grading or teaching styles, or if the students in the classes taught by the English lecturer simply performed better.

Another failing of our study was the decision to give students the option of meeting with either a librarian or writing tutor based on their own personal preference. The majority of students chose to meet with a writing tutor, which left us limited results on how the library and librarian component contributed to student success.

Due to many of these discrepancies, challenges, and lessons learned, we decided to run a second phase of our study with significant adjustments based on what we learned during the first study. This time around we are working with English 102 Composition II: Research and Reasoning classes. While English 101 afforded us the opportunity to work with a standard syllabus, we realized that the focus on research in English 102 made it a better fit for our services. Additionally, this meant we could work with English faculty as opposed to English teaching assistants, which increased the reliability of the instructors we worked with. During our AiA project, we ran into communication issues. This time, however, we made sure that we met with all of the English instructors prior to the start of the survey. We also stayed in continual contact with them to make sure everyone was clear on their responsibilities and expectations for participating in the study. We also decided to specifically recruit English instructors who were teaching two sections of English 102 to participate in our study. This way we would have a class taught by each instructor in the control group and the test group. We ended up with four instructors participating for a total of eight classes divided evenly.

About halfway through our first project, we realized that tracking students for one quarter was not enough and we added additional modes of tracking students after the fact. With our second run of the study, we designed our project to track students for a full year. We decided to integrate the ARC into English 102 in Winter 2015 and then continue to track the students through Spring 2015 and Fall 2015 quarters. For the purposes of tracking students, we decided to continue with the self-assessment model. We once again requested that students self-assess their comfort with academic writing and research. We also inquired if they visited the ARC during Spring/Fall Quarters and if they met with a librarian or tutor. We also asked if the student had been required to meet with a librarian or tutor in conjunction with a class.

We continued to collect grades for the course and final paper but in our second study we took this a step further. The grades were a good start but it did not provide us with a way of truly assessing the impact we made on the classes that participated in our study. Also as I previously mentioned, the grading was inconsistent between sections. As a way of better assessing our impact on students, we decided to collect final papers from all eight English 102 sections—and evaluate the papers using a rubric. The rubric will examine source choice and citations. We are excited about this addition and believe that with the changes and adjustments we have made, we will have a very strong assessment study.

Overall our study provided us with positive results and we were able to track a correlation between the integration of the ARC into English 101 and final course grades. We also saw that students in our test group reported they were more likely to visit the ARC again and meet with a tutor and/or librarian in the future than those students in our control group. Our test group reported higher confidence levels for academic writing and research. However, as previously mentioned there were some unanticipated challenges with our original study that we sought to correct with our new study. If I could provide any advice for future library assessment projects, it would be to communicate effectively and often with the participants in your study to be sure that everyone is clear on the expectations and time-lines. I would also suggest being open to changing your assessment project as you move through the research process. The information you learn at the beginning of an assessment study can influence and shape the scope and structure of your study and may ultimately lead to a better assessment project in the end.

Further Reading

Cook, Douglas and Lesley Farmer. *Using Qualitative Methods in Action Research: How Librarians Can Get to the Why of Data.* Chicago: Association of College and Research Libraries, 2011.

Creswell, John. *Research Design: Qualitative, Quantitative, and Mixed Methods Approaches* (4th ed.) Thousand Oaks, CA: SAGE Publications, 2014.

Fowler, Floyd. *Survey Research Methods* (4th ed.) Thousand Oaks, CA: SAGE Publications, 2009.

Services

CHAPTER 20

Library Research Consultants:
Measuring a New Service

Mary O'Kelly

Grand Valley State University
okellym@gvsu.edu

IMAGINE YOU WORK IN a little beach-side shopping district filled with boutiques, charter fishing, and cafés. You own the ice cream shop—all the other owners are your friends and neighbors. One storefront is owned by a long-established, high-budget company with multiple locations. One is a small, local start-up. Others are seasonal, opening and closing depending on the time of year. Each is independent, with an independent budget and timeline. Suddenly the city planner wants to know whether your well-loved, charming corner of town is really contributing to the economy. Is it really making a difference in the lives of people who visit and work there? Are tourists more likely to recommend that their friends visit? Do they like this section of the beach better than others? Are your workers content with their skills and opportunities? *How would you measure success?*

Such is the dilemma of measuring shared services. Grand Valley State University Libraries offers students 'one-stop shopping' for research, writing, and oral presentation assistance as components of a collaborative academic support service called the Knowledge Market. The University Libraries has a goal of being the central academic hub of the campus. To that end, we started the Knowledge Market, a partnership with the Fred Meijer

Center for Writing and Michigan Authors (commonly called the Writing Center) and the Speech Lab. The library also hosts the Office of Undergraduate Research and Scholarship, the Office of Fellowships, and the IT Helpdesk. While not part of the Knowledge Market, these campus services are highly visible and active collaborators. Several other support services have also asked to join the library in various types of formal and informal relationships: Student Academic Success Center (a.k.a. the tutoring center), the Chemistry department tutors, and the brand new Data Inquiry Lab.

Just as in our busy little beach town, each of these services has independent budgets, staffs, and timelines. They have their own stated learning objectives. We all share a common mission to support student learning, but our methods vary. Our outcomes vary. Necessarily, so do our assessments.

Success is contextual. Our Assessment in Action (AiA) project originally was designed to measure all three Knowledge Market services: library research, writing, and speech. We all want our students to succeed academically. What does that mean? It can mean that they stay in school (retention and persistence), that they get good grades (high GPA), or other recognition for their academic work (scholarships, grants, publications, fellowships). It can mean that they are confident, independent learners who believe that they are in control of their own achievements (self-efficacy). More specifically, it could mean that they are able to measurably demonstrate their mastery of information literacy skills and concepts, their adherence to best practices in writing, and their effectiveness in communicating orally. This only scratches the surface of the variables influencing a multi-partner academic service in a multi-location library system serving a comprehensive university of 25,000 undergraduate and graduate students. In short, it's complicated.

Choosing a Method

Our AiA project coincided with the opening a new, $65 million library and the launch of the Knowledge Market. Early meetings with partners focused on general operational policies and procedures rather than assessment. By necessity, each of our program evaluation practices began to develop independently based on the reporting and funding requirements of our three administrative units. This was complication number one in assessing a shared support service.. Because of this, each service proceeded with their own independent assessment. We all agreed that shared assessment is an important goal but that such a complex project for a new service would require a significant amount of time, and during that first year time was in short supply.

The first step for the library was to identify what we wanted to know. By starting with a list of clear questions we were able to identify specific measures that would provide us with answers. In other words, the questions led us to the methods. For example, we wanted to know the grade point average (GPA) of students who met with a research consultant compared to students who did not. This seemed simple enough on the surface but it ended up involving multiple steps and departments. We wanted the GPA, which means we needed the identity of each student who had a consulting appointment. We then needed the mean and median GPA of these students and the mean and median GPA of all students who did not meet with a consultant during the year so we could compare those numbers. Library staff do not have access to student grades, so this required the assistance of the campus Institutional Analysis department. They could access the student data and report it back to the library in aggregate and stripped off all identifying information.

Ultimately we devised twenty-three questions§ that guided our measurement of indirect student engagement with the research consulting service. We gathered data employing a mixed methods approach that included using surveys with Likert scales, multiple choice questions, and open-ended comment boxes; qualitative analysis of notes from consultants on the content and outcome of each consultation; quantitative analysis of student academic data; and exploration of theoretical models of peer learning.

Unfortunately we were unable to obtain any direct measures of student learning. This would have required negotiation and planning with classroom faculty who had students come to the consultants for specific assignments. This process simply was not built into our AiA project. However, the project helped us articulate a tangible need for direct measures and gave us a template for designing future assessments. We offer what has become a key academic support service on campus and it is essential that we collect evidence that demonstrates how our service influences student learning.

---

§ For information about the specifics of the instruments used in our project, please contact the author.

Limitations and Findings

We had huge ideas for our AiA project. I was the only library representative; everyone else was from the other services, so many of our project team's early meetings were spent debating the disciplinary-specific languages of "research" and "program evaluation" and "student learning assessment" in information literacy, writing, and communication rather than settling into a unified assessment plan.

Early on we abandoned the idea of directly measuring student learning for the library research consultations due to the time limitations. It couldn't be done in one semester. Students come to the Knowledge Market for help with a specific course assignment. Naturally, we would need cooperation from the professor and permission from the student to see the final assignment. These complexities led to us step back from shared assessment of all three services, back from measuring student learning, and instead give ourselves permission to measure only our service.

We found significant value in those evaluations we did undertake and the resulting statistics. We know, for example, how many students had a consultation, at what time of day, and in what location, all of which we used to modify our scheduling. We also know the students' majors and in which courses they wanted help. We looked for patterns and informed the appropriate liaison librarians. This enabled them to have timely and relevant conversations with professors: "Over a dozen of your students came to the Knowledge Market for help with the literature review you assigned. I'd be happy to come to class in the next week to provide additional support." Identifying scheduling and assignment patterns alone helped improve the service.

In the past academic year (2014-2015), 98.65% of students completed a three–question evaluation form as part of a required check-out process. Students reported that they felt comfortable with the consultant (93% very comfortable), found the service helpful (78.6% very helpful; the rest found it somewhat helpful), and felt more confident completing an assignment after meeting with a consultant (98.28% very confident). These were self-selected students who recognized a need and chose to avail themselves of this academic support service. We have identified many variables that can influence self-reporting and, while the evaluations did help us evaluate the consultants and consultations, we recognize that feeling good about the service is quite different from learning something from it.

This learning process inspired us to add assessment of student learning to the library's new three-year assessment cycle. We put a priority on figuring out how to assess student learning because of the limitations of self-reported evaluations and simple descriptive statistics.

Community Resources

The relationship we formed with Institutional Analysis was the single most important outcome of our project. Their research and analysis staff offered us invaluable expertise that we just could not replicate in the libraries. They have access to rich student-level data that, we hope, will eventually help us find a correlation between consultations and retention, consultations and student learning, library instruction and retention, library engagement and persistence to graduation, and so on. Institutional Analysis is able to keep that data private and secure, and they have the analytical skills to ensure that our findings are based on solid, reliable statistical methods. While participation in AiA certainly enhanced my own capacity for designing and managing major assessment projects, it also taught me that part of being a good project manager is reaching out to community resources in order to elevate the capacity of the whole team.

Lessons Learned

If I had it to do all over again, I would have started small. I would begin with our library's strategic plan and build one (not twenty-three) very solid and very attainable inquiry question. I would plan my team based on the specific expertise each person could bring: one or two instruction librarians, one representative from Institutional Analysis, one from the campus assessment committee, and one from another peer-consulting service on campus. I would spend more time learning and documenting the process of assessment and less time worrying about our findings. I would draw on our simplified experience to create a replicable process that could be used in the library to help build a well-informed culture of assessment.

There is a certain external credibility that comes with involving a library leader in a national effort to build assessment capacity. I used that to open doors to new discussions and to build new relationships. Perhaps most importantly, I have been able to more effectively for information literacy on campus. I deeply believe that the academic library is an essential academic support service and now we are gathering evidence to back up that belief with facts.

Throughout this process I learned how to manage an assessment project to completion. I learned the language of assessment and how to communicate our results using relevant, targeted messages. The project gave me the opportunity to not only build my own assessment skills but also to specifically measure our new peer research consulting service and make meaningful improvements to the service based on our results. It also taught me to take time at a project's conclusion to reflect on what worked and what didn't so that future projects are even better.

Recommendations for Assessing a Peer Research Consulting Service

Measuring the success of in-library academic support services can be complex, and even more so if the whole evaluation process is new. Keep the following in mind:

- **Define success:** First, figure out what success means to you.
- **Limit the scope:** For your first assessment project focus only on the library, even if you have other consulting partners (such as the writing center) working with you. You can always take what you learn from the first project and apply it to more ambitious projects later.
- **Be thorough and consistent with data collection:** If you want to measure specific student outcomes, find a way to accurately and consistently gather student identification and notes about the assignment from every single consultation.
- **Ask for advice:** Get a group of interested people from the library and ask them what *they* want to know about the service. Their questions may inspire a whole new set of assessment priorities.
- **Plan your process:** After you have formed your questions, ask what data you need to answer those questions, how you will get the data, how you will analyze it, and who needs to know the results.
- **Network:** Reach out to others in a similar situation. Find librarians who are partnering with writing centers or who manage an information commons. Offer to share what you learn.

- **Build your own support network:** Find the institutional analysis department on your campus and ask for support.
- **Communicate the right message to the right audience:** Break your findings apart and share the appropriate pieces with different audiences. Give liaison librarians information to share with their departmental faculty—they will be significant allies in helping you build a consulting service with direct ties to the curriculum.
- **Remember the consultants:** Evaluate whether the consultants themselves are learning. They are students too and stand to benefit significantly from their work.
- **Give student employees an opportunity to contribute:** Share findings with the consultants. Even better, let them help with the analysis and write-up. Give them ownership of some of the communication. Perhaps they can design an informational poster or create a video targeted at fellow students. They can be your strongest advocates.
- **Reflect:** Most importantly, use the opportunity to learn something about yourself.

Further Reading

Bodemer, Brett. "They CAN and They SHOULD: Undergraduates Providing Peer Reference and Instruction." *College & Research Libraries* 75, no. 2 (2014): 162–78.

Bruffee, Kenneth. "Collaborative Learning and the 'Conversation of Mankind.'" *College English* 46, no. 7 (1984): 635–52.

Bruffee, Kenneth. "Peer Tutoring and Institutional Change," in *Collaborative Learning: Higher Education, Interdependence, and Authority of Knowledge,* 82–83. Baltimore: Johns Hopkins University Press, 1993.

Deese-Roberts, Susan and Kathleen Keating. *Library Instruction: A Peer Tutoring Model.* Englewood, CO: Libraries Unlimited, 2000.

Faix, Allison. "Peer Reference Revisited: Evolution of a Peer-Reference Model." *Reference Services Review* 42, no. 2 (2014), 305–319.

Falchikov, Nancy and Margo Blythman. *Learning Together: Peer Tutoring in Higher Education.* New York: Routledge/Farmer, 2001.

Harris, Muriel. "Talking in the Middle: Why Writers Need Writing Tutors." *College English* 57, no. 1 (1995): 27–42.

O'Kelly, Mary, Julie Garrison, Brian Merry, and Jennifer Torreano. "Building a Peer-Learning Service for Students in an Academic Library." *portal: Libraries and the Academy* 15, no. 1 (2015): 163–182.

Schendel, Ellen, Julie Garrison, Patrick Johnson, and Lee Van Orsdel. "Making Noise in the Library: Designing a Student Learning Environment to Support a Liberal Education," in *Cases on Higher Education Spaces: Innovation, Collaboration, and Technology*, ed. Russell Carpenter, 290–312. Hershey, PA: Information Science Reference, 2013.

Stanfield, Andrea, and Russell Palmer. "Peer-ing into the Information Commons." *Reference Services Review* 38, no. 4 (2011) 634–46.

CHAPTER 21

Dedicated Technology Facilities:

Impacts, Success, and Implications

Eric Resnis

Miami (Ohio) University
resnisew@miamioh.edu

AS TECHNOLOGY PLAYS AN ever increasing and vital part of student engagement and scholarship, Libraries have developed spaces to accommodate these needs.

These dedicated technology spaces such as Information Commons, provide students with the software, hardware, and expertise needed to complete both basic and complex projects. Assessment of these spaces has traditionally been based solely on usage, including users per time period or number of software uses. However, as library assessment culture continues to mature, matching student success to these rooms is necessary.

Miami University is a public university with a main campus in Oxford, Ohio (approximately 40 miles northwest of Cincinnati). In 2015, the main campus had an undergraduate enrollment of approximately 16,000 students and a total graduate enrollment of 1,900 students. The university is residential and focuses primarily on undergraduate liberal education. The Oxford campus supports the King Library (the main library), and three subject-based satellite libraries: Art and Architecture Library, Music Library, and the Business, Engineering, Science, and Technology (BEST) Library.

The Libraries have long been considered a campus forerunner in implementing new technologies that support student learning. The Center for Information Management (CIM) opened in 1998, an early example of the Information Commons model. The room has evolved considerably since that time, but its primary function remains unchanged: to provide students with access to sophisticated software that is not widely available in other areas on campus. Dedicated staff support is also available to users, and workshops are regularly offered on technology packages that are available in CIM. Positive response to the facility resulted in the inclusion of a similar facility, named the Digital Den, when the BEST Library was built in 2011.

Assessment of the spaces until recently was based primarily on gate counts and software usage statistics. While these numbers are helpful in figuring out how the room is used and maintaining appropriate offerings of software packages, these figures do not tell us how the facilities are truly supporting students. This was what prompted us to apply to be part of the Assessment in Action (AiA) community—to figure out how to begin looking at this important piece of assessment for our technological facilities.

Our research question for the project was considerably broad: How does the usage of our dedicated technology facilities contribute to the success of Miami student scholarship and research? Our AiA project was intended to explore a range of possible projects which would help to answer our research question. The intent was that we would continue to build upon these projects after AiA with revised and additional projects that could help to answer the research question.

Our AiA campus team, consisting of myself, the Associate Provost for Undergraduate Education, the Director of the Center for the Enhancement of Teaching, Learning, and University Assessment, and the Assistant Director of the Office of Institutional Research, decided that we should consider two projects: one using an indirect assessment method, and the other using a direct method. The indirect method we chose was Technological Self-Efficacy (TSE), the belief in one's ability to successfully complete a technologically-related task. We utilized the work of Deborah Compeau and Christopher Higgins[1] in creating a Technological Self-Efficacy survey that not only looked at the nature of technological use (software familiarity, proficiency, and utility), but also usability of the room and the support therein.

During a two-week medium-volume period, users of CIM and the Digital Den were presented with an optional two-question survey when they logged into a machine:

1. What do you plan to work on today?

2. If this is for a class, which one?

Each user was presented with these questions only once, no matter how many times they used the facilities during that time. This initial survey was also given to users of facilities without the same level of technology and service: the Kamm Instruction Room in King Library and other computers on the first floor of the BEST Library. Users completing the initial survey were then asked to complete a longer questionnaire on their technological self-efficacy. Some questions in which students were asked to rate themselves include:

- Using the software enables me to accomplish the task more quickly.
- I could not have completed the task without this software.
- Using this room helped me to better complete this task.

Our direct method of choice was examining the visual literacy of posters presented at our annual Undergraduate Research Fair. We chose this project for two reasons: 1) we had strong anecdotal evidence of providing assistance to students before the event in previous years, and 2) we hoped to create a new and lasting partnership with the Office for Undergraduate Research, which was to move into King Library a few months after the study was complete. For the study, we developed a rubric that was based on the visual literacy rubrics from Quinnipiac University and Texas A&M University.[2] The rubric evaluated five aspects of visual literacy, two concerning poster design, and three pertaining to explanation of the poster:

- Interpreter—Meaning: Student can describe overall meaning of the poster.
- Interpreter—Parts/Whole: Student can describe how certain elements of the poster contribute to the whole.
- Interpreter—Design: Student can describe their design process.
- Creator—Product & Content: Content of the poster.
- Creator—Design: Design elements of poster.

Three reviewers were trained in use of the rubric which was normed utilizing a process from Holmes and Oakleaf.[3] We surveyed participants beforehand to see if they had used CIM/Digital Den, and then samples were created for each of the three poster sessions that contained a mixture of posters where students utilized CIM/Digital Den, and students who did not. Five posters for each session were reviewed by two reviewers to account for reviewer bias during the statistical analysis. A total of 60 posters were reviewed during the research fair. The implementation of both assessment methods were conducted mostly by library staff, although we did partner with the Office for Undergraduate Research to obtain the names of students who were participating in the Undergraduate Research Fair.

Our methods related well to the research question, though as mentioned earlier, we were only looking at a small part of the overall question. The following criteria indicate what we hoped to see:

- Students who use CIM/Digital Den have higher levels of technological self-efficacy than those who do not.
- Students count CIM/Digital Den resources as a major factor in their level of computer self-efficacy.
- Students who use CIM/Digital Den are more confident in using digital technologies than those who do not.
- Students who use CIM/Digital Den have a higher level of visual literacy than those who do not.

Each assessment method had its limitations; some were known during the design phase, and others become apparent when we were analyzing results. For the TSE project, the sampling time period was somewhat of a limitation. As the initial survey was somewhat invasive (popping up during login to a computer), we decided to sample during a time of medium-activity rather than high-activity. We also decided to configure the survey so that no user would see it more than once, no matter how many times they logged in during the sampling period. There was concern that implementation of the survey during a high-period of activity such as mid-terms week or the weeks approaching finals would result in undue additional stress on students. We were also concerned that implementation during a high-activity period would result in a lower response rate. Our reasoning seemed to hold up after implementation was complete. We had a response rate of 46.3%, with no complaints from users about the survey. However, software package usage during this period was fairly basic, with 67% of users indicating they were using a web browser or Microsoft Office suite product. Our existing data (usage statistics) indicate that usage of more sophisticated software such as Adobe InDesign, Dreamweaver, ArcGIS geospatial software, and other packages tends to be higher near exams periods. As this type of software is the true hallmark of CIM and Digital Den, it would have been helpful to have a larger sample of users in the final analysis.

Another limitation of the TSE study was the choice of a control location. We chose the Kamm Instructional Room in King Library and first floor machines at BEST Library (outside of the Digital Den, which is also located on the first floor) as we thought they had the most differences in software offerings. However, most of our respondents utilized software that was available in both CIM/Digital Den *and* the control locations, so it was not possible to use location as a determination in TSE values as we had hoped.

Microsoft Office and web browsers have always been available on all library computers. Additionally, over time some more sophisticated software such as Adobe Photoshop has also migrated to computers located outside of CIM/Digital Den. While we were able to reframe the results to make a case for using CIM/Digital Den to help foster student success when using sophisticated software packages,[4] the data did not give conclusive evidence about the impact of the rooms. In the next iteration of our study we will need to be very careful about selecting a control location that significantly minimizes overlap in software between the control and CIM/Digital Den. We will also need to adjust instrument questions somewhat to better capture student perceptions on the impact of the CIM/Digital Den.

For the visual literacy study, one limitation resulted from the data that was gathered beforehand, which we used to create sampling groups. This data was somewhat difficult to obtain, and there was error in communicating our questions to students who were presenting at the research fair. As a result, we knew whether students used CIM/Digital Den or not, but we did not know the nature of their usage (i.e., whether they were using CIM/Digital Den for the purposes of this poster or some other activity). A second limitation was the nature of the item assessed. While the visual literacy study is easily replicated, the assessment occurs only one day a year. Our local team felt that it was beneficial to assess an item that is not tied to any given class and had representation from all disciplines and most departments. However, examining artifacts over the course of a year may have created for a more efficient workflow.

The last limitation (and whether it truly was a limitation) was discussed extensively by our campus team before and after implementation: the rubric itself. We chose a visual literacy rubric that examined both the artifact and the person creating the artifact. This did create a limitation as discussed in the prior paragraph, as we had to conduct assessment on the day of the research fair, and could not collect artifacts for assessment at a later time. It could also be argued that the rubric was limiting in that it focused somewhat more on the in-person aspect (three categories) than the artifact itself (two categories), and that it might have been better to develop a rubric focused more, or solely, on the artifact. However, the team felt that we were assessing visual literacy holistically, and that students talking about their poster help to inform us greatly on the nature of the artifact itself. While the services in CIM/Digital Den are more focused on tools and assistance in creating the artifact, they are also imparting visual literacy knowledge, which could be called upon when discussing the poster with others. Visual literacy of the artifact and the description of the artifact are not mutually exclusive skills.

For others who are considering using similar methods, I can offer several suggestions. The first, which was always forefront in our minds, was to determine whether the chosen assessment methods truly and purposefully assist in answering the inquiry question. Also, think very carefully about all possible extenuating circumstances and intervening variables, and how they might interfere with your study and/or analysis. It may be impossible to think about every possibility, but completing due diligence is essential. This is an area where we could have done better, and tweaked our implementation procedures in order to have more conclusive results. Additionally, think about your control very carefully.

My final suggestion is to never forego norming of a new rubric or a rubric that is new to any evaluator. Our norming process was very long and involved, even though we only had three evaluators. Consensus initially was very difficult on all the posters we examined, but improved with time. However, I am certain that without norming, we would have had completely useless data.

My AiA project utilized two disparate methods for the same inquiry question, which leads to my final point: there is a multitude of ways to assess this type of inquiry questions. For direct assessment methods, the key is to find a project/assignment that utilizes the space purposefully, and attempt to compare it to a similar situation for engagement with the space does not occur. This could be webpage projects, illustrative projects, and movies just to name a few. Other literacies could be examined, and creating efficiencies with information literacy assessment is certainly possible. For indirect assessment methods, any type of survey is possible depending on the aspect of service you are examining.

Notes

1. Deborah R. Compeau and Christopher A. Higgins, "Computer Self-Efficacy: Development of a Measure and Initial Test," *MIS Quarterly* 19, no. 2 (1995): 189–211.
2. "Quinnipiac University Visual Literacy Essential Learning Outcome Rubric," Quinnipiac University, accessed May 31, 2015, http://learn.quinnipiac.edu/eportfolioinfo/rubrics/Visual_Literacy_Rubric.pdf; "Texas A&M University Student Leader Learning Outcomes Rubrics," Texas A&M University, from http://sllo.tamu.edu/rubrics, accessed May 31, 2015.
3. Claire Holmes and Megan Oakleaf, "The Official (and Unofficial) Rules for Norming Rubrics Successfully," *Journal of Academic Librarianship* 39 no. 6 (2013): 599–602.
4. Eric Resnis, "Assessing Student Technological Self-Efficacy," (Miami University Assessment Brief #84, May 19, 2014), accessed May 31, 2015, http://www.units.miamioh.edu/celt/assessment/briefs/Brief_84.pdf

Further Reading

Armenteros, M., Shu-ShengLiaw, M. Fernandez, R. Flores Diaz and R. Arteaga Sanchez. "Surveying FIFA Instructors' Behavioral Intention toward the Multimedia Teaching Materials." *Computers & Education*, 61 (2013): 91–104.

Blakesley, David and Collin Brookes. "Introduction: Notes on Visual Rhetoric." *Enculturation*. 3, no. 2 (2001). Accessed June 19, 2015. http://enculturation.net/3_2/introduction.html

Deborah, R., Darren B. Meister and Christopher A. Higgins. "From Prediction to Explanation: Reconceptualizing and Extending the Perceived Characteristics of Innovating." *Journal of the Association for Information Systems* 8, no 8 (2007): 409–439.

Kher, Hemant V., James P. Downey and Ellen Monk. "A Longitudinal Examination of Computer Self-Efficacy Change Trajectories during Training." *Computers in Human Behavior* 29, no. 4 (2013): 1816–1824.

Marks, Diane. "Literacy, Instruction, and Technology: Meeting Millennials on Their Own Turf." *AACE Journal* 17, no. 4 (2009): 363–377.

CHAPTER 22

Filling in the Venn Diagram:

Second Year Students, Research, Writing

Susan E. Montgomery

Olin Library, Rollins College
smontgomery@rollins.edu

Suzanne D. Robertshaw

Olin Library, Rollins College
srobertshaw@rollins.edu

THE OLIN LIBRARY AT Rollins College in Winter Park, Florida researched second-year students' use of our various services as they worked on their research projects. With the recent move of the Tutoring and Writing Center (TWC) to the library, we decided to explore our combined value to student learning. We were interested in finding answers to these questions:

- Where were our students including us in their research and writing process?
- How do our students transfer their research skills in advanced classes?
- How could we ensure that both the library and the TWC were not merely co-located, but genuinely collaborating in our students' learning?

Our project targeted second-year students as part of the recent campus-wide dialogue about supporting students after their first year—one of very intentional guidance and mentoring. After more than ten years of providing extended orientation as part of new-students' first-semester courses, with peer mentor, faculty, and staff advising built in, the College was evaluating the state of support for students who decided to return to our university. We knew that librarians provide instruction at the request of the course professor to students assigned a research project. They also offer one-on-one assistance either at the research help desk or in their office. We also knew that peer tutors and writing consultants primarily offer individual help to students seeking assistance. For this research on the value of our departments to students' academic success, we needed either numbers, or data, as well as individual stories: the big picture and the idiosyncratic one.

Our methods followed from these questions and from what information we and our campus partners such as Institutional Research and the Division of Student Affairs normally collect. Library circulation data revealed what students checked out. Library instruction sessions helped us determine what courses librarians had taught but not who received the instruction or how they used the information in their learning. Due to privacy concerns, research-help transactions did not reveal who asked the question or for which course the student needed assistance. In contrast, TWC sessions with peers gave us very specific numbers for students, courses, frequency, and length. Institutional data gave us course enrollments, names and numbers. Initially we expected Information Technology (IT) to provide us with numbers of interactions or enrollment in their short courses. Student Affairs could share insights about student life from student surveys in MAP-Works administered by the Office of Student Success. In addition to this quantitative data, we wanted to obtain detailed explanations of students' learning, research, and writing processes. We conducted ethnographic interviews with ten second-year students about their idiosyncratic processes in their previous research projects. We used NVivo in the transcribed interviews to compare processes and reveal points of assistance students obtained.

We wanted to see the use of library services by students in their second-year of attendance at Rollins, as they were progressing in their studies past the first year. Information about these students was initially hard to isolate. Students are identified in our system as freshmen, sophomore, junior, etc., based upon credit hours earned. For sophomore standing, students need to have completed at least 30 semester hours, and the college organizes data on students accordingly. We learned that many second-year students could either be registered as juniors, if they arrived with more credits due to Advanced Placement exams or other college level courses taken prior to enrollment (as with many tutors) or as freshmen, if they did not satisfactorily pass a course during their first year on campus. We had to get help from the college's Institutional Research office to identify students by "Admit Year" to the college rather than by academic level.

Since the data maintained by the library follow the preferred institutional format, we could only determine from our records how sophomores, not second-year students, used our services. Data was generally limited because libraries do not maintain records of individual user activity as a matter of privacy. Nonetheless, our library's circulation records for the Fall 2013 semester did show that sophomores checked out equipment such as headphones, computer chargers, laptops, etc. Not surprisingly, they checked out more books than freshmen but at a lower rate than juniors or seniors. Records of research help interactions gave us different data, still not sufficiently substantive for even more reasons. We could only determine the number and the level of interactions between the librarian and the user—1 (easiest), 2 (somewhat challenging), or 3 (most challenging). The research help data did not specify who was asking the question or for what specific course.

Finding relevant and substantive data about our "one-shot" library instruction sessions for second-year students was also challenging. During the Fall 2013 semester, our librarians taught 23 in-class research sessions to courses enrolling second-year students. We were unable, however, to confirm how many second-year students received this library instruction since these classes did not restrict enrollment to second-year students. Furthermore, some could have been absent the day of the library instruction class.

Unlike the library, the TWC could isolate data for second year student use. For that same semester, Fall 2013, 270 first-year students made appointments. Slightly fewer second-year students, 213, did so. As students advanced academically, they went to the TWC less frequently; third- and fourth-year students made the least number of appointments. We could determine which courses the target group had come for help in, the purpose for the student's appointment—a paper or a project or something related.

The quantitative data we collected from both the library and TWC gave us only half the picture of how second-year students use our services in their learning. We decided to gather qualitative data as a way to obtain a better understanding of our research pool. We chose to conduct interviews with ten second-year students who had three commonalities: all were in their second year of attendance at Rollins, all had completed a paper requiring outside research, and all had received in class library instruction from a librarian. We wanted students with different majors and with corresponding distinct research experiences. We hoped for all the students to have had TWC appointments, but we had to loosen that stipulation so as not to limit our research pool. In the end, fortunately, all but one had made appointments at the TWC.

It was extremely challenging to isolate a diverse group of students who met the criteria. We identified more than ten students but had difficulty contacting them for interviews. Students did not readily respond to the campus emails inviting them to participate in our research. Our $10 incentive "for an hour of your time" did not lure students as we anticipated. We benefited from using Facebook, the popular social media site, to find several students who agreed to be interviewed. The Coordinator of the TWC knew one student personally and asked her to participate. One interviewee offered to contact another student whom we wanted to include in our study. That student agreed to be interviewed shortly afterwards. One student who perfectly met our criteria flatly refused. Initially we thought we could complete the interview process within a month or two, but the delay of contacting and arranging the interviews with the students prolonged our research schedule. We also had to receive Institutional Review Board (IRB) approval before beginning the interviews. While not difficult, it added another step to the process. We did not expect the process of identifying students to interview and coordinating the actual interview to be so challenging. Going forward, we know that any future research projects involving interviewing students should abide by the idea of "doubling the time" we expect for initial steps to be completed.

It took almost two semesters to complete the interviews with all ten students. We based our interview questions on previous ethnographic interviews as reported in *Participatory Design in Academic Libraries* and in the ERIAL project.[1] Transcription of the interviews took several months and then we used NVivo software to analyze the interviews. Fortunately, our college had recently purchased a subscription, but we needed to learn how to use the software, a time-consuming task. It was worth it, since NVivo gave us the deep analysis which highlighted common themes in our students' research and writing processes as well as times when they turned to us or others for help.

This research gave us the needed data to share with our campus community about how students use the library and the TWC in their learning. The limitation of conducting student interviews as part of our research was that it was specific to our campus population and to our course demands. We had considered reviewing bibliographies from student papers in lieu of student interviews, but the interviews described the student's process in research, seeking help, and completing the assignment, none of which the bibliographies would have revealed.

To gauge how much these ten students remembered about effective searching techniques in the research process, we had them conduct a mock search on a pertinent topic in their major. We captured their process on the computer as they searched, to complement their self-reported answers about how they found appropriate sources in their research process. We learned that used the same resources they had discovered in their 100-level courses, often from our initial library instruction sessions, rather than trying more specialized databases. An Education major conducted her search in a general multidisciplinary database rather than choosing a subject specific one like ERIC. (A more thorough report of our process and results can be found in our associated article.[2])

Our Assessment in Action project provided us with the opportunity to begin discussing ways for the library and the TWC to start working together to support our students' learning. The TWC moved into the library in January 2013 and outside of co-presentations between librarians and the Coordinator of the TWC, our departments were not effectively working together. We could see students using both of our services but only had anecdotal evidence of how they actually used them. We capitalized on the AiA program to delve deeper into our students' research and writing process. Our plan is for our two departments to continue working strategically to help students understand the overlaps between their research and writing processes. We will emphasize the importance of incorporating both the library and the TWC to ensure our students' academic success.

Notes

1. Marilyn Pukkila and Ellen Freeman, "Co-Viewing: Creating Broader Participation Through Ethnographic Library Research," in *Participatory Design in Academic Libraries: New Reports and Findings*, Nancy Fried Foster ed., (Washington, DC: Council on Library and Information Resources, 2014), 55, http://www.clir.org/pubs/reports/pub161/pub161.pdf; "ERIAL Interview Guide Questions," in *College Libraries and Student Culture: What We Now Know*, Andrew D. Asher and Lynda M. Duke eds., (Chicago: American Library Association, 2012), 170–172.
2. Susan E. Montgomery and Suzanne D. Robertshaw, "From Co-location to Collaboration: Working together to improve Student Learning," *Behavioral & Social Sciences Librarian* 34, no. 2 (2015): 55–69.

Services

CHAPTER 23

Research Assistance Linked to Student Retention

Linda Bedwell

Dalhousie University Libraries
lbedwell@dal.ca

WHEN WE AT DALHOUSIE University in Halifax, Nova Scotia first heard about the Assessment in Action (AiA) program, we had just discovered that our student retention rate was the lowest in the U15 (Dalhousie's peer group of top fifteen research-intensive universities in Canada). Instead of measuring the effect of current services on retention, we undertook a literature review and decided to create a new "intervention" type of service. The plan was to identify a group of at-risk students and create a program of mandatory Research Assistance (RA) specifically for them. We considered several potential student groups. Our pilot project eventually focused on a small, specific set of at-risk students: readmitted students in the Faculty of Arts & Social Sciences (FASS). These students were academically dismissed after their first year, appealed their dismissal, and were granted conditional re-admittance to the university.

Settling on program design and assessment methodology was challenging. We acknowledged at the outset that this would be a learning experience and that in the end the effort was for a good cause. We labeled our Dalhousie Libraries Research Assistance Program (DLRAP) as a "seed project." This meant the program was fledgling, and through assessment and support would grow and improve over time.

Why did we specifically choose to implement an RA program for re-admitted, at-risk students? Like most things, it started with a hunch. We had a feeling, based on our interactions with students while providing RA, that we are doing a good thing. By assisting them with research related to their graded research papers, we are teaching them how to effectively source and evaluate scholarly material so they can produce better papers and succeed academically. Also, it seems that in this RA role, we are like the "bartenders" of campus. Students talk candidly to us about their academic work and their experiences in university. Afterwards they seem to walk away relieved and rejuvenated. With this hunch that we are establishing personal connections with our students and helping them succeed academically through RA (and how could this not lead to better chances of retention?), we reviewed the extensive literature on retention. From this we gathered two takeaways: 1) academic success is the strongest factor affecting a student's decision to remain at university, and 2) it is important that students develop personal connections with members of the institution. This confirmed our choice of creating a mandatory program for our readmitted FASS students to participate in, something we already did on a regular basis: RA. Our next step was to determine how we would assess the impact of the RA on the retention of these students.

Choosing the Methodology

Academic success can be defined and measured in many different ways. At one point, it was suggested to us that we only focus on grades of research papers, rather than overall grades (i.e., GPAs). We felt that the impact of obtaining information literacy skills (as students do during RA sessions) has far-reaching beneficial effects beyond the writing of a single research paper. Plus a grade on a one-time research paper didn't give us a starting point from which to measure impact. We wanted to measure *improvements* in grades, not grades in general. Using GPAs also provided us with a natural "control" group: the readmitted students who did not participate in the program (we couldn't really enforce the "mandatory" measure). We did acknowledge that there was only so much we could control for in this group—more on that later. Therefore we decided to measure the average change in GPAs, from the last year to the end of the current academic year. With that data we could then compare the changes in GPAs of those who participated in the RA program and those who did not.

We also chose to survey the participating students by asking them if they felt the RA program benefited both their grades on their specific research papers, as well as on their overall grades (or GPA). The results would provide some triangulation to the GPA analysis. With the survey we could also tackle the assessment of the personal connection that we felt that the one-on-one RA gave the students.

There are several ways of asking the participating students these questions. We could have held focus groups or conducted individual interviews. However, given the sensitivity around academic performance we felt the need to protect the students' privacy regarding this rather personal issue. An online survey was preferable to a focus group which placed the students together in one room and required them to reveal to others that they had failed their first year of university. Gathering these students together in one physical location at the end of the academic year we felt would also be a challenge. Alternatively we could have conducted interviews. As we found when we were registering and scheduling RA appointments with these students, they were very difficult to get in touch with.

In the end, it was an online survey that we went with. Most of the survey questions were open-ended, even if the question could be answered with a general yes or no. We wanted to allow the students the opportunity to say anything. The survey was emailed to each student with the plea that it was our first year to run this program and we really needed their feedback. The survey served the assessment purpose, but also allowed us to gather suggestions on how to improve the program. In the end, we gained so much insight out of this survey!

How Did It Go?

Overall, both the GPA and survey assessment methods were suitable and effective, given the limitations of our project. The survey received a good response rate with over half the twenty-five RA participants responding. Although the survey target group was small, being a seed project meant that we were only looking for results *compelling enough* to support growing the project. We achieved that goal. Since most of the survey questions were open-ended, the results required some qualitative analysis—coding of the results. As it was a small respondent group this was an easy task.

The last question on the survey asked how else the RA program affected the student and her/his studies. The students surprised us. Despite being an open-ended question, there was considerable consistency in their responses. Over half of them stated that the program gave them confidence. This was an effect we hadn't really thought of. Knowing that our students are walking away from RA sessions with us feeling confident to do their work, gave us more reason to continue the good work we do. It also echoed the findings I later read in First Year Experience literature: confidence fluctuates in a student's first year and can have a significant impact on their academic activities.[1] Had we anticipated a significant increase in confidence as a potential side-effect, pertinent to the retention of students, we may have measured it as a closed-ended, multiple choice or scale question. It is something we will consider when we run the program again in 2015–16.

Another thing we will consider is not making the survey anonymous. As we analyzed the responses, we felt it would have been helpful to know a little more about the respondents. Which respondents had the highest GPA increases? Which respondents attended both RA sessions (there were two); which attended only one? (We kept track of all this information separately.) Which ones came with assignments in hand, upon which to base the session? (We found that a third did not and this correlated with lower GPA changes.) If we want to keep the survey anonymous, it will at least be helpful to conduct two surveys: one after the first RA session, and one after the second.

The survey was also helpful in that it provided triangulation on the question of whether or not the RA sessions impacted their GPAs. By the students indicating in their survey responses that the sessions did so, it gave strength to the correlation shown in the GPA analysis. The GPA analysis showed that those who attended both RA sessions improved their GPA more so than those who attended no sessions (an average increase of .371 vs. .196). Note that the GPA analysis revealed a correlation, not causation. From reading the retention literature we know that there are a multitude of compounding factors affecting a student's ability or choice to remain at their studies at their institution. Since our study cannot control for many factors affecting academic success, we can't test for causation. So for now our assessment will have to rely on correlation, not causation.

While many of us work for educational institutions where research is very important, we have to remind ourselves and others that assessment is not research. We aim to live up to the rigors of research, but we are measuring things not in a lab, but in real, messy, complicated life. We knew at the outset of this project that we simply could not control for the myriad of factors that affect both academic success and also a student's personal connection to their university. However by providing evidence compelling enough, we could grow this project and with each successive year add to this persuasive body of evidence.

Recommendations

The first year of our DLRAP program for readmitted FASS students was followed by my sabbatical, so DLRAP was not repeated in the 2014-15 academic year. We documented our lessons learned and how we would do things differently the next time. At the time of this writing, we are preparing to conduct DLRAP for the coming academic year (2015-16). I am revisiting our recommendations, accompanied with new knowledge based on some sabbatical research, membership on campus-wide retention strategy teams, and attendance at my first First Year Experience Conference.[¶] My first major recommendation for Dalhousie going forward and to other libraries considering a similar assessment project: have your institutional research (Analytics) office assist you or take over any analysis of GPAs. At the time of the DLRAP project, our Analytics office did not have the resources to help us. The office has since expanded and I will be making use of their expertise. Within their institutional databases, they can most effectively track grades and record various student data, including involvement in campus programs. The Analytics office will also employ approved methods for accounting for changes to past GPAs as the result of repeated courses. They may be able to advise on better quantitative assessment methods as well as have access to term grades and other relevant student data. The Analytics office may also make it possible to track survey responses by student IDs mapped to level of participation in the program. There's a lot this office can do that I am not able to, due to lack of expertise, access to data, and privacy restrictions.

¶ I recommend this conference to librarians interested in developing programs or in simply getting involved in campus-wide retention efforts.

The results of our assessment study showed that those who had assignments upon which to base their RA session improved their GPAs, whereas those who did not flat lined with no improvement at all. Therefore, I recommend working with faculty in the courses taken by the participating students to develop research assignments. These need not be lengthy, but at the very least be a challenge to the students. This will allow the students to experience "earned-success", and receive RA from us that resonates with their academic work. At the time of this writing, we have developed a partnership with a campus-wide remedial program that most of the readmitted FASS students will be taking. We are designing an assignment to be administered in the program for which the readmitted students will base their first RA session on.

As discussed earlier, we are going to consider intentionally measuring the effect DLRAP has on the students' confidence in a survey. We are also currently planning on running two surveys—one after each of the two RA sessions—to effectively measure the impact and gather feedback on each session separately. We will know soon enough if this was an improvement to our assessment methodology.

Overall, larger numbers are more compelling. With the success of DLRAP's first year, we must expand on the program. Currently, we are repeating it with FASS, but interest in it is growing from Dalhousie's Engineering retention office. Larger groups of participants means more data. Especially when it comes to correlation, larger data sets and repeated correlation makes for a more compelling argument to support your service. We also need to track both the participants and control groups to degree completion—whether they complete their degree at Dalhousie and the number of years it takes them.

In conclusion, assessment of library services is essential. This is particularly true if the service is fledgling and needs to be "sold" to library or university administration for support and resources. I hope our experiences doing so with a project we feel is for the greater good will help you with yours.

Notes

1.   Community College Research Center (CCRC), "I Came in Unsure of Everything: Community College Students' Shifts in Confidence," by Susan E. Bickerstaff Melissa Barragan, and Zawadi Rucks-Ahidiana, CCRC Work-

ing Paper No. 48 (New York, NY: Teacher's College, Columbia University, September 2012), accessed September 9, 2014, http://academiccommons. columbia.edu/catalog/ac:153122

Further Reading

Australian Survey of Student Engagement (AUSSIE). "Dropout DNA, and the Genetics of Effective Support." By Hamish Coates and Laurie Ransom. AUSSE Research Briefings 11. Camberwell, VIC: Australian Council for Educational Research, June 2011. Accessed September 9, 2014. http://research.acer.edu.au/cgi/viewcontent.cgi?article=1000&context=ausse

Bell, Steven. "Keeping Them Enrolled: How Academic Libraries Contribute to Student Retention." *Library Issues* 29, no. 1 (2008): 1–4.

Blackburn, Heidi. "Shhh! No Talking about Retention in the Library!" *Education Libraries* 33, no. 1 (2010): 24–30.

Cox, Rebecca D. ""It Was Just That I Was Afraid: Promoting Success by Addressing Students' Fear of Failure." *Community College Review* 37, no. 1 (2009): 52–80.

Hagel, Pauline, Anne Horn, Sue Owen and Michael Currie. "How Can We Help? The Contribution of University Libraries to Student Retention." *Australian Academic & Research Libraries* 43, no. 3 (2012): 214–230.

Johnson, Judith L. "Commuter College Students: What Factors Determine Who Will Persist or Who Will Drop Out." *College Student Journal* 31, no. 3 (1997): 323–332.

Pascarella, Ernest T., John C. Smart and Corinna A. Ethington. "Long-Term Persistence of Two-Year College Students." *Research in Higher Education* 24, no. 1 (1986): 47–71.

Pascarella, Ernest T. and Patrick T. Terenzini. *How College Affects Students*. San Francisco, CA: Jossey-Bass, 2005.

Sander, Paul and Lalage Sanders. "Understanding Academic Confidence." *Psychology Teaching Review* 12, no. 1 (2006): 29–42.

Tinto, Vincent. *Leaving College: Rethinking the Causes and Cures of Student Attrition*. Chicago, IL: University of Chicago Press, 1987.

CHAPTER 24

Methodological Issues:
Assessing the Impact of Using the Library on Student Success at the University of Northern Colorado

Annie Epperson

University of Northern Colorado
annie.epperson@unco.edu

METHODOLOGICALLY, THE ASSESSMENT IN Action (AiA) project at University of Northern Colorado's James A. Michener Library was an experiment that drew upon the expertise of the librarian team leader, the two campus team members, and the staff and faculty colleagues of the librarian team leader. The major focus of the project was to answer the research question initially posed as: "Does using the library facility enhance student success?" This was a year-long, wide-ranging project that incorporated mixed methods and showed results with varying degrees of success.

Selection of Methods

The final project included quantitative and ethnographic practices to gather data to address the research question. Mixed methods were deemed appropriate in order to explore the three components of the research question, including 1) what extrinsic and intrinsic motivators bring students to use the library, 2) are students who are active in co-curricular activities also users of the library, 3) what are faculty expectations for student use of the library, and how does that expectation manifest itself in actual student use. Specifically, the project included focus groups, a furniture use survey, and a new method developed for this research, the video booth interview. In addition, quantitative data such as GPA was collected on those who participated in the focus groups and video booth interviews, and specific questions relating to the research were added to the annual graduating senior survey and the biennial faculty survey.

Inquiry Question Operationalization

The project focused on the library as a place on campus, with a core question of "Does using the library facility enhance student success?" Because of the complexity and breadth of the question, the team broke that question into subcomponents in order to identify sources of data that could address each, as outlined in Table 24.1 below.

TABLE 24.1. OPERATIONALIZATION OF THE INQUIRY

COMPONENTS OF THE CORE QUESTION	SOURCE OF DATA/METHOD OF COLLECTION
Faculty & staff expectations that use of the library facility (Michener Library) increases student success.	Additional of questions on the Faculty Survey.
Student expectations for a library visit—what needs are being met, or not?	LibQual data; focus group; additional questions on the Senior Survey.
What areas of Michener are most popular for student use? What aspects of the facility influences use of a particular space (type of seating, noise policy, presence or absence of books) over time of day?	Furniture use survey; focus group; video booth.
What aspects of the Michener facility influence student use of the facility (affective value of spaces)?	Focus group; video booth.
How do students use the spaces and resources within the facility?	Furniture use survey; video booth.

TABLE 24.1. OPERATIONALIZATION OF THE INQUIRY

COMPONENTS OF THE CORE QUESTION	SOURCE OF DATA/METHOD OF COLLECTION
What motivates students to use the library (self, instructor, group, resources, etc.)? Once IN Michener, what motivates them to use resources or particular spaces?	Focus group; video booth; .
Who uses the library, and why? Who does NOT use the library, and why?	LibQual data; Senior Survey.
Do students who use the library also engage in co-curricular activities?	LibQual data, focus group; video booth; Senior Survey.
Does use of the library influence GPA and graduation rate?	LibQual data, Senior Survey, GPA (of those who participate in focus groups and video booth).

It became clear that even with this level of detailed inquiry, the question can only be partially answered. Places and furnishings within the library can be identified as preferred and contributing to *(self-reported)* academic success. Definitive results however cannot be connected to student success as measured by retention and GPA. This is primarily because of the small sample sizes in both the focus groups (n = 7) and the video booth interviews (n = 18).

Limitations of the Methods

Each method employed had limitations, including those that are familiar to social science researchers. The focus groups and video booth interviews required significant investments of resources to recruit sufficient numbers of participants. Any data drawn from institutional records are dependent on sufficient numbers of data points to be meaningful. Focus groups and interviews also yield qualitative data which can be challenging to analyze. Finally, the furniture use survey data collection phase involved training and supervising nearly a dozen student workers.

External Assistance with Implementation

In addition to the two campus team members, a graduate student research assistant helped recruit focus group participants and conducted the focus group sessions. As team leader, my limited training in focus group methodology prompted me to seek a more experienced individual. In addition, best practices in interactive qualitative methods suggest that the individual leading focus groups should be somewhat removed from the topic at hand, in order to minimize bias or contamination of the data,[1] so this was an added benefit of working with someone outside of the project team. The graduate research assistant had no direct connection to the University Libraries and thusly could easily maintain an objective presence. This individual also performed an initial examination of the focus group data in order to identify themes and help formulate questions for the video booth interviews, the next step in the data collection phase.

Leveraging institutional data necessitated conversations with the Office of Assessment and the Information Management & Technology (IMT) unit. Assessment personnel assisted in the formatting and analysis of additional questions placed on the annual Senior Survey and biennial Faculty Survey. The IMT provided to us data such as GPA and status information for those individuals who participated in the focus group and video interview booth interview components.

All other personnel involved in the project were drawn from the University Libraries. Several faculty, staff, and student workers assisted in the implementation of the furniture use survey and the video booth interview components.

Suggestions for Implementing these Methods

This project incorporated two novel methods that are a bit unusual: the furniture use survey and the video booth interview. Both are useful in their own ways, and I'd encourage others to consider using them. The furniture use survey takes perceptions of how patrons use space, including what they do, preferred seating and location within the library, from the anecdotal to the level of quantifiable evidence. In this particular case, because the building is so large and open so many hours in the course of a week, it was prudent to sample, rather than undertake a complete census. Analysis of the data also presented the opportunity to think critically about the types and placement of furnishings used within the library.

The video booth interview was a surprise, being fairly easy and fast to implement, and yet providing a wealth of rich qualitative data. In two hours' time eighteen participants answered three highly-focused questions. Since the method collected both audio and video data, body language and other non-verbal signals contributed to a greater understanding of the respondents' message. Analysis of this data closely resembled examination of interview or focus group data, allowing for more nuanced results.

Possible Alternative Methods

It would be interesting and possibly enlightening to implement a more anthropological method similar to the work of Nancy Fried Foster at the University of Rochester[2] to learn more about the role that use of the library plays in student academic success. Since one of the most significant challenges to our particular project was the limited generalizability due to the small sample size, it seems obvious to incorporate more qualitative methods. However, in a different setting at a larger institution, for example, or with a team member more suited to the subtleties of statistical analysis, a more quantitative project may have greater success.

Conclusion

This ambitious project used mixed methods to explore what impact use of the library facility has on student academic success. Because of the complexities associated with operationalizing that central question of library use, a multiplicity of methods was needed to address its three components: motivation(s) to use the library, the impact of faculty expectations, and the relationship between library uses and participation in co-curricular activities. A strong team from the outset was critical to the success of the AiA project, as was the support of colleagues in the library. The original method of video booth interview data collection was both fun and interesting. Others are encouraged to experiment with this new method as an alternative to focus groups or interviews.

Acknowledgments

This project was part of the program "Assessment in Action: Academic Libraries and Student Success" which is sponsored by the Association of College and Research Libraries (ACRL) in partnership with the Association for Institutional Research and the Association of Public and Land-grant Universities. The program, a cornerstone of ACRL's Value of Academic Libraries initiative, is made possible by the Institute of Museum and Library Services.

The author wishes to express gratitude to Dean of Libraries Helen I. Reed and Associate Dean Gregory Heald for their encouragement and support of AiA project implementation at University of Northern Colorado's James A. Michener Library. Many thanks also go to colleagues who assisted with the project: Sara O'Donnell, Jessica Hayden, Wendy Highby, Kendra Spahr, Diana Gunnells, David White, Andy Malinski, Kalen May, and Diana Algiene-Henry. The following individuals were of immense assistance: Kim Black and Randall (Jr.) McGrath in the Office of Assessment, and Liz (Kimberly) Gilchrist, doctoral candidate in the Counselor Education and Supervision program. The students who participated in the focus groups and video booth interviews provided a wealth of data along with their time. Finally, the project would not have taken the shape that it did without the thoughtful input and continued good humor of campus AiA team members Evan Welch and James Henderson.

Notes

1. Earl Babbie, *The Practice of Social Research* (Belmont, CA: Wadsworth, 1998).
2. Scott Carlson, "An Anthropologist in the Library," Technology, *The Chronicle of Higher Education*, August 17, 2007, A26, accessed May 22, 2015, http://chronicle.com/article/An-Anthropologist-in-the/22071

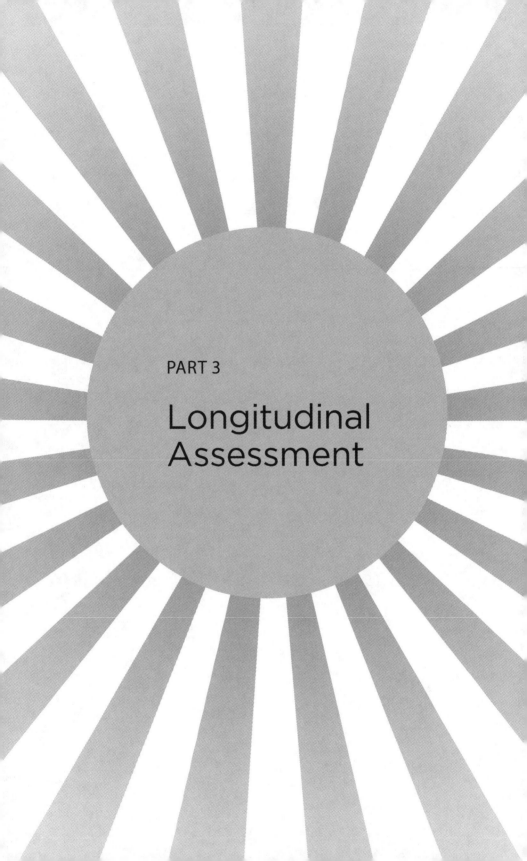

PART 3

Longitudinal Assessment

CHAPTER 25

Known Library Use and Student Retention:
A Methods Case Study

Ashley Ireland

Waterfield Library, Murray State University
aireland@murraystate.edu

AT MURRAY STATE UNIVERSITY we developed our Assessment in Action (AiA) project to serve two markedly different needs. One the one hand the University Libraries sought to answer the call to action in ACRL's *The Value of Academic Libraries: A Comprehensive Research Review and Report* and develop methods that directly assess library impact on metrics like enrollment, retention, student success, student learning, and others regarding faculty productivity or institutional prestige.[1] We knew for instance that we had the means and drive to contribute to the ongoing conversation at Murray State on declining student retention. However library assessment measures have traditionally involved counting things used, isolated from the user (e.g. item circulation, use of electronic resources, etc.). We therefore had no methods in place to address a possible relationship between student use of library space or resources and retention to graduation.

On the other hand the Libraries sought to leverage creative means in building its donor base. At Murray State the Libraries have a dedicated development officer, but our donor pool was limited to alumni who had majored in library science—a program with a limited lifespan at Murray

State. We considered the argument that *all graduates are library graduates* to be a strong one, the administration of the Development Office largely disagreed. Alumni of each program were "owned," so to speak, by their respective colleges, and those colleges served as primary contacts for donor development among them. However alumni could be tagged as potential donors if they fell within specific populations. In order to tag alumni as potential library donors we needed a definitive method to identify library users.

In order to address both of these issues we needed to build a massive dataset of known library use tied to individual users. An inquiry question and methodology were already largely developed before we even applied to participate in AiA. The project was timely. We were able to leverage the credibility that came with our participation in this nationally-recognized ACRL/IMLS effort toward improving academic library assessment measures toward institutional buy-in. The nature of our project dictated the composition of the AiA team: the Director of User & Instruction Services, the Dean of Libraries, and the Systems Coordinator represented the University Libraries; other members of the University community included the Director of Student Retention, the Director of Institutional Effectiveness, and a faculty member from the Department of Psychology who served as+ methodologist.

We started with a list of metrics that could potentially be tied to individual library users: circulation stats, interlibrary loan requests, library computer lab log-ins, use of the writing and communication centers housed in the main campus library, use of electronic resources, participation in library instruction sessions, and enrollment in the Libraries' credit-bearing course. Early in the development of the project the primary goal was to lay the groundwork for compiling one large dataset. We designated users' University-assigned institution numbers (known as M Numbers) as unique identifiers. While the Writing and Communication Centers were gathering usage statistics and participant names, we directed them to begin capturing M Numbers as part of the appointment scheduling process. M Numbers for students enrolled in our credit-bearing courses were discoverable in the course management system. Logins to our campus network, including those through our library computer labs, employ a username serving as a user's email address which can be easily run through the patron database to obtain M Numbers. Our staff incorporated the M Number into the ILLiad interlibrary loan request form years ago. Gathering other metrics though required significantly more preparatory work.

At the project's inception Murray State Libraries was using Ex Libris' Voyager as its integrated library system. The circulation module does not retain user circulation history once an item has been returned, in order to protect user privacy. Voyager does however count circulations per user. It was determined that we could capture a circulation count for each year by capturing all the counter figures for each unique user at the beginning of the academic year and comparing it to the figures available at the end of each semester. Any change in the counter meant that the user had borrowed *something*. This might include anything in our physical collection including traditional books, media, and other items such as laptops, headphones, and even iPods. This was not a problem for us; the circulation metrics simply reflected a certain level of student-library engagement.

Library instruction requires significant staffing, scheduling, and outreach support. Murray State has developed a scaffold of instruction for each academic program enabling us to teach to appropriate formative and summative learning objectives appropriate to the course level and discipline. This effort is however largely. Instruction librarians may meet with students once or twice in a semester. They do not grade student work and often do not have an opportunity to even get the names of the students that may ask detailed questions. In order to include the library instruction element in our dataset we needed a way of capturing the identity of users in the classes we instructed. We discussed passing around sign-in sheets in class to get M Numbers but this was ruled out. We wanted to rely on unobtrusive measures of data collection if possible so as to minimize the possibility of disrupting user behavior. Sign-in sheets would have been time consuming for library instructors and would have likely meant reducing the amount of time spent teaching. Therefore we decided to record the registration numbers of the each of the courses for which we conducted instruction sessions and request an enrollment list from the Registrar at the end of the semester. While this metric was highly predictive of student retention we cannot say which students were actually present during library instruction. We knew that going in but deemed it the least obtrusive method available.

The metric that generated the most discussion and debate was measuring the use of electronic resources. Before developing our AiA project the

University Libraries had no sense of the number of unique users driving the use counters for these resources. The Systems Coordinator informed us though that the proxy server we used to authenticate off-campus users of electronic resources was capturing unique user data based on Active Directory. One possible means of aligning electronic resource use to unique users would be pushing all traffic for those resources, including all databases, electronic journals, and ebooks, through the proxy server. Naturally this raised concerns about user privacy; the Director of User & Instruction Services and the Dean of Libraries presented our proposal to library faculty and department heads in a series of meetings that thus occasioned serious conversations. We were, after all, considering changing procedures for the purposes of gathering information on our users. We defended the proposed changes by pointing out that specific search queries or resources utilized were not included in the information that would be gathered. There was also concern however that the proxy login would be an unnecessary hassle for *on*-campus users. In the end the tremendous information-gathering potential of our strategy combined with the added benefit of more efficient troubleshooting of login issues (those of us on-campus would have the same online experience as those off) won us the day. Consensus was reached at last and at the start of the next semester we began authenticating all users of electronic resources through the proxy server.

After settling on our study's scope and methodology, it was determined that we should discuss the project with the Institutional Review Board. It wasn't clear to us whether this step was necessary as we were gathering data intended for institutional assessment, but we knew that part of the AiA process included presenting on methods and findings at the American Library Association Annual Conference. I presented our plan to Murray State's IRB Coordinator who refused to even consider approving the project without approval from the Registrar. She had serious reservations about such a far-reaching data project that involved gathering information on library users, even if the goal was to better understand those users. She expressed concern about centralizing such data for analysis, particularly because of the value libraries place on user privacy. The meeting with the University Registrar had an altogether different tone; she asked detailed questions about the security of the data and insisted that the centralized dataset would be anonymized by the Registrar's Office when they added additional demographic information. We took this approval back to the

IRB Coordinator for review and received IRB approval for the project shortly thereafter.

The infrastructure we put in place worked throughout the semester and at its conclusion the Systems Coordinator was to combine all the library use elements in a Microsoft Access database using the student M Number as the common identifier. Each library use element was simply coded as a 1 or 0. A 1 indicated that a student used the resource at least once during the semester and a 0 indicated no known use. No frequencies were captured; it didn't matter to us how many items were checked out or how many times an individual logged into the proxy server. Even once was enough to suit our purposes.

The file was saved to an external hard drive that was always held in a locked drawer in a locked office. Once all the known library use elements were part of the file the entire dataset was delivered to the Registrar's Office for the addition of demographic information. I did not expect this step to be difficult, but it turned out to be. We requested roughly twice as many data points as were returned. It turns out an element such as full-time or part-time is not easy to capture, as it may change at some point during the semester. We therefore had to specify that we were interested in the students' status at the end of the semester rather than the beginning. Our institution does not tag students as main-campus or distance students because, for instance, a student living in the dorms might well register for an all-online semester of courses. We were thus left with gender, year of birth, race/ethnicity, academic rank the previous semester, major, and retention from one semester to the next. There were even issues with the retention element due to its being interpreted very literally; we initially interpreted the data as indicating the University failed to retain a significant number of its seniors, only to realize that graduating seniors had been tagged as "not retained". Once we were able to talk through the specificity of the data elements requested and do a little cleanup we had a dataset that included *all* Murray State students in our assessment. The Registrar removed the M Number from the file before returning it to us for analysis.

The methodologist on the project employed standard statistical analysis methods to investigate the relationship between known library use and student retention. The results were just what we had hoped for. We found strong positive relationships between many of our elements and even some interesting negative relationships that were easy to explain when controlling for certain demographics. As an example, there was a negative relationship between use of our Writing Center and retention into the next semester. This indicates that our Writing Center serves the most at-risk students and that use alone isn't enough to predict retention. Further, the Writing Center is heavily used by international students participating in our ESL program rather than a traditional academic program. International students may visit Murray State to complete a certain level in the ESL program and never take main campus courses.

While the study was successful in demonstrating relationships between known library use and student retention, at this point they only reflect the experience at Murray State and, in particular, the experience of the students enrolled for the duration of the study. We believe however that there is great potential for this largely new method of compiling previously existing data to analyze empirically the relationship of libraries to a campus-wide imperative.

Murray State continues to gather these library use metrics for future analysis. We hope to add an additional element in the near future: reference transactions. Reference transactions represent some of the most personal work we do with our users as one has to confess to some ignorance in order to request help. We hope to start gathering email addresses as part of our reference interview process in order to facilitate follow-ups, and these emails may be conveniently added to our large dataset. We also hope to clarify the somewhat misleading circulation metric. Because our laptops and other technology are barcoded, those particular library uses are counted as a circulation rather than use of the computer lab. We must better rethink the circulation of technology which may be eased by the transition to a new ILS in the coming year. We also hope to compare our results to similar datasets from other institutions.

There have been very successful studies of similar scope at the University of Minnesota,[2] Curtain University in Western Australia,[3] and the University of Huddersfield,[4] but this project was undertaken at a regional public institution rather than a research institution and included unique elements. Ultimately we want forward-thinking librarians at similarly-sized institutions to know that this is a scalable project that can be implemented without significant changes in workflows. We also want to encourage some change in the typical assessment of academic libraries where effectiveness is often broadly defined by gate counts, reference questions, database queries, and limited replicability of learning following information literacy instruction. We want university administrators to expect more from academic libraries and give them a seat at the table where imperative metrics are discussed. As institutions and their units transition to performance-based funding it is imperative that academic libraries be able to communicate the direct or indirect impact of library space, services, collections, and staffing on student retention and success.

Notes

1. Megan J. Oakleaf, *The Value of Academic Libraries: A Comprehensive Research Review and Report* (Chicago, IL: Association of College and Research Libraries, American Library Association, 2010).
2. Krista M. Soria, Jan Fransen and Shane Nackerud, "Library Use and Undergraduate Student Outcomes: New Evidence for Students' Retention and Academic Success," *portal: Libraries and the Academy* 13, no. 2 (2013): 147–164; Krista M. Soria, Jan Fransen and Shane Nackerud, "Stacks, Serials, Search Engines, and Students' Success: First-Year Undergraduate Students' Library Use, Academic Achievement, and Retention," *The Journal of Academic Librarianship* 40, no. 1 (2014): 84–91.
3. Gaby Haddow, "Academic Library Use and Student Retention: A Quantitative Analysis," *Library & Information Science Research* 35, no. 2 (2013): 127–136.
4. Deborah Goodall and David Pattern, "Academic Library Non/Low Use and Undergraduate Student Achievement: A Preliminary Report of Research in Progress," *Library Management* 32, no. 3 (2011): 159–170.

CHAPTER 26

Assessment Archaeology:
Digging Up Old Data for Longitudinal Assessments

Alison Bradley

University of North Carolina at Charlotte
adbradle@uncc.edu

Stephanie Otis

University of North Carolina at Charlotte
sotis@uncc.edu

ASSESSING LONG-TERM EFFECTS OF library instruction on student success would typically require a longitudinal study that takes several years to design, implement, and complete. After identifying the outcomes to study, appropriate metrics would be gathered over a span of years, with final analysis and evaluation to follow. When the first cohort of Assessment in Action (AiA) was organized, our team decided to explore the historical data we had available at the time to try and conduct a retroactive longitudinal study, investigating long-term effects that participation in freshman library instruction had on our students but in a study designed to fit within the fourteen month time frame of the program.

In 2012, the University of North Carolina system's Board of Governors directed each of the 16 campuses to focus on improving success in student retention, persistence, and graduation rates, along with efficiency overall.

Campus priorities for assessment at the University of North Carolina at Charlotte (UNC Charlotte) have therefore shifted. Departmental funding is no longer allocated based upon head counts and enrollment statistics, Instead it is based on the number of students retained from year to year, and the number that graduate within four or six years of enrollment. Library assessments have historically consisted of simply counting numbers of classes taught and students in attendance. However, the AiA program presented an opportunity to design new assessments that would align with the new focus on student outcomes and success required from other academic units. The professional literature shows evidence of library contact increasing student engagement and success (see "Further Reading" below), and our project was designed to search for concrete evidence of this connection at UNC Charlotte.

Our AiA team was recruited to address the changing priorities on campus. From the library, the group included the library's Instruction Coordinator and the Head of Research and Information Services. We also invited two campus partners to broaden the knowledge and expertise of the team: the Assistant Provost, who serves as the campus point person for initiatives related to student learning outcomes and assessment, and an analyst in the Office of Institutional Research (IR), who has access to all student records within a secure and confidential database. The Assistant Provost guided our selection of metrics and outcomes to analyze by sharing her first-hand knowledge of the priorities held by the Provost, Chancellor, and other campus leaders. Including an analyst from IR as a member of the team from the beginning of the project allowed the technical aspects of our data analysis to be refined and improved upon throughout the project. His familiarity with the database structure of available student records as well as his understanding of the depth of analysis possible allowed us to select robust outcomes like GPA or fall-to-fall retention without violating student privacy or confidentiality. This group balanced technical ability, institutional leadership, and front-line library experience to develop a substantive assessment of library impact that stayed focused on the most current institutional priorities.

This project was designed to find ways to demonstrate a relationship between the library's instruction program and the student success metrics that are driving campus policies. Our methods of assessment were selected to complement our project's emphasis on campus priorities, and to satisfy the practical issues that arose from that emphasis. Any study of retention and graduation rates must be longitudinal, which forced the project team to think creatively about how to conduct even a pilot study within the mandated 14-month time frame. Generating and collecting enough new data to test our question within the project timeline was impossible, so we needed to work creatively to conduct a longitudinal analysis. Our focus for the duration of the project, then, was how to mine and analyze existing data, even though historically the library's data collection hadn't been designed with this type of analysis in mind.

Our project was originally designed to map the participation of undergraduate students in library instruction, comparing students who are reached through library instruction with those who are not. Using library statistics and data from the IR, we planned to look for patterns in student success and retention among students receiving course-based library instruction. Our initial research question was simple: investigate whether students who received library instruction as undergraduates are retained fall-to-fall at a higher rate than the overall first-time full-time freshman population.

The greatest challenge in implementing our project as designed was the quality of available data to analyze. In our initial planning stages, we had hoped to analyze the previous six years of library instruction, using the lists of course sections that scheduled library instruction to evaluate the progression of students to graduation within four or six years, the standard benchmarks for our campus and state university system. As we began gathering instruction statistics, though, it quickly became clear that records were too incomplete for us to confidently identify the cohort of students who had received library instruction. Statistics on classes taught had been gathered in three different systems over the six year span, and turnover had been high in the library instruction team. This gap in our records led us to decide that we should narrow our focus to a specific large-scale course, with data that could be consistently reconstructed. The best statistics available for tracking multi-year effects were for University Writing (UWRT) courses. Since a typical fall semester of UWRT includes over 120 sections of first-year students, taught by thirty or more instructors, the library's Instruction Coordinator maintains a detailed spreadsheet of sections assigned to the various members of the library's UWRT instruction team. By comparing the original spreadsheet assignments to the statistics submitted by each librarian, and confirming with comparison to the library classroom booking records, we were able to confidently recreate the list of sections of UWRT that had received in-person library instruction and a complementary list of those that did not.

After the AiA library team members compiled lists of sections that received library instruction, the IR team member ran an analysis to see if the students enrolled in these sections showed any variation in semester-to-semester retention as compared to students in UWRT sections that did not receive in-class or online library instruction. Overall, the variations seen were small and inconclusive. Small patterns that emerged did reinforce changes in the UWRT library instruction program that had been made by the Instruction Coordinator over recent years. In particular, the lack of connection (or slight negative correlation) between library instruction and student success measures in the earliest introductory courses served to confirm the decision to eliminate face-to-face library instruction for those courses. Though our data and methods did not fully address our original question, going through the process of recreating clean data for analysis from a variety of historical sources allowed the library team members to bring back recommendations to the rest of the instruction team on how to best prepare for this type of study in the future.

The biggest drawback to our approach was that the data that was clean and complete enough to use addressed only a single, narrow point of contact that the library makes with students. Retention is informed by student engagement, and library engagement is an interesting and complex part of that broad picture. Our methods, due to the limitations of our data, did not address or account for that complexity. We would recommend that future library researchers consider carefully how well their data aligns with the effect they intend to study. In this instance, we used a very narrow, specific intervention (reaching students through library instruction in UWRT) to assess a broad effect (retention and progression to graduation). This mismatch of scope is likely to cause problems in future studies. A better plan would be to collect and analyze a wider range of ways that the library engages with students, and search for patterns of retention and progression within that broader picture. Retention and progression to graduation are too all-encompassing to be assessed as effects of narrow and precise interventions. Instead, the library's role must be established by using as many points of contact with the student as possible. Effective and accurate collection of student data at the point of library engagement will be essential to demonstrate any effect on student success. Since campus assessment priorities are changing to privilege these complex outcomes, the library has an opportunity to stay engaged if we shift our own focus and collect a broader range of data as well.

For our library and our campus, taking this first step and running the study did have practical benefits. By working closely with the Assistant Provost to discuss how campus priorities were changing, the library is now better prepared to establish our role in meeting campus goals. As we worked with IR to run the analysis of our existing data and statistics, we learned how best to gather data for easy, confidential analysis of student outcomes in the future.

While we recommend careful consideration in matching available data to realistic outcomes, we would also encourage moving forward with pilot assessment efforts when the opportunity arises, rather than waiting in hopes of developing the best possible study. We found value in pursuing our project even without an exact match between our methods and our question. An imperfect assessment project still offers the advantage of opportunities to participate in campus assessment conversations, of practice at applying research methods to our work, and of sparking library-wide conversations about developing robust assessment projects. Although existing instruction statistics were not complete enough to effectively assess retention and progression to graduation, we did learn how easily we can partner with IR to evaluate those metrics with any set of students we can identify, without having to worry about privacy and confidentiality concerns. What we have learned positions us to demonstrate to colleagues the ways we could use a wide range of data we collect in our day-to-day operations for comprehensive assessments of student success.

Sharing the results of this project with the liaison librarians showed them how keeping accurate statistics can help us demonstrate our own role in student success, as well as helping position them as assessment partners with their assigned colleges and departments. Sharing the results of this pilot and the IR workflow with other library units has encouraged them to begin planning ways of securely tracking the success of students who use library services. In spite of some obstacles, our experience with AiA has been valuable given the reality of data-driven decision making and resource allocation in higher education. This project has helped prepare us with the tools we need to demonstrate our value to our colleagues as well as our campus partners and leadership.

Further Reading

Bell, Steven. "Keeping Them Enrolled: How Academic Libraries Contribute to Student Retention." *Library Issues* 29, no. 1 (September 2008).

Blackburn, Heidi. "Shhh! No Talking about Retention in the Library!" *Education Libraries* 33, no. 1 (Spring 2010).

Gilchrist, Debra and Megan Oakleaf. "An Essential Partner: The Librarian's Role in Student Learning Assessment." *National Institute for Learning Outcomes Assessment—Occasional Paper #14* (April, 2012).

Haddow, Gaby and Joseph Jayanthi. "Loans, Logins, and Lasting the Course: Academic Library Use and Student Retention." *Australian Academic & Research Libraries* 41, no. 4 (2010): 233–244.

Oakleaf, Megan, Michelle S. Millet and Leah Kraus. "All Together Now: Getting Faculty, Administrators, and Staff Engaged in Information Literacy Assessment." *portal: Libraries and the Academy* 11, no. 3 (2011): 831–852.

Rodriguez, Derek. "Understanding Library Impacts on Student Learning." *In the Library with the Lead Pipe* (blog), June 15, 2011. Shulman, Lee S. "Counting and Recounting: Assessment and the Quest for Accountability." *Change: The Magazine of Higher Learning* 39, no. 1 (2007): 20–25.

Upcraft, M. Lee and John H. Schuh. "Assessment vs. Research: Why We Should Care about the Difference." *About Campus* 7, no. 1 (March–April 2002), 16–20.

Whitmire, Ethelene. "Academic Library Performance Measures and Undergraduates' Library Use and Educational Outcomes." *Library & Information Science Research* 24 (2002): 107–128.

CHAPTER 27

Impact of Library Usage on Student Success:
Exploring New Territory

Aaron Lupton

York University
aalupton@yorku.ca

YORK UNIVERSITY LIBRARY'S (YUL) Assessment in Action (AiA) project was inspired by the "Discovering the Impact of Library Use and Student Performance" project undertaken by the University of Wollongong, which aimed to produce data that could reveal a correlation between students' grades (success) and use of the library to demonstrate the impact of the library on student success.[1] YUL does not have an Assessment Librarian but does have an Assessment Committee. The Committee was looking for assessment projects by means of which we could demonstrate the library's value, especially after hearing about similar projects at the 2012 Library Assessment Conference. Furthermore one of York's Associate University Librarians had already engaged in conversations with members of OIPA (Office of Institutional Planning and Analysis), York's institutional research office. The OIPA was looking for projects that could demonstrate how various units at York were contributing to the university and adding value.

There was much discussion within the Assessment Committee about the form our project could take. In the University of Wollongong example the library used EZproxy logs as their measurement unit for library use. The EZproxy logs reveal each time a user accesses electronic resources from off campus, including databases, e-books, and eReserves.[2] In another, similar project at the University of Minnesota several measures of library usage were used including "circulation data, online resource usage records, workstation login data, workshop registrations, and more".[3] However at York we were very limited in terms of the data that we could access. We knew the number of times books were borrowed but could not access the student information associated with transactions. We did not collect student IDs at the reference desk and we did not record student attendance for library instruction classes. Meetings with LCS revealed that EZproxy logs were kept, so we knew we at least had access to this data. The EZproxy logs contained student IDs and it would be a relatively simple process for our OIPA analyst to trace these IDs to the individual GPA and anonymize the data. Our ultimate form our inquiry question took was "what can we learn about the impact of the library on student success by examining use of eResources and student GPA?"

We knew that there were several limitations and unknowns for this experiment, not the least of which was the knowledge that using an electronic resource cannot actually translate to student success—there was no causal link between using an electronic resource and a grade. However it was felt that simply looking at a correlation between library usage and GPA would at least have some value. It would allow us to quantify a positive relationship between the library and student success, which is something the library has not been able to do in the past. Normally when the library would describe its value it was through narratives concerning the importance of the library in student life and learning. However accurate the narratives, to be able to *quantify* the library's contribution to student success in some way would be considered an accomplishment. Of course we had no idea what the analysis would reveal, but we still considered it a worthwhile experiment.

There were some significant challenges to obtaining the data, including the EZproxy logs themselves and the subsequent data analysis designed to reveal any correlation between usage and GPA. We had planned to begin our analysis in spring 2013 but due to delays in obtaining the EZproxy logs from LCS, partly due to privacy concerns in obtaining and using student data, we did not get the data until July 2013. Having the Provost's support of the AiA project proved useful in convincing LCS to provide the data.

By the time we obtained the data, priorities at OIPA had shifted and this project was no longer high on their list. It took months of follow-up to convince OIPA to begin the analysis. Originally our sample size of EZproxy logs was to comprise seven years of usage, covering all users. To make the analysis more manageable we reduced the sample size to all first-year students for the 2012/13 academic year.

The result of this change in sample size led to a realignment of the project's purpose. We were no longer measuring the impact of the library on all users but first year students. Since first-year experience was a strategic priority of the university, as expressed in York's First Year Experience (FYE) Framework,[4] there was a shift to align the AiA project with FYE. The Framework does very little to address the role of the library, so the project could at least help fill that gap.

Ultimately the analysis performed by OIPA involved adding library usage to a preexisting model of first-year student success. Typically OIPA used high school performance as the best predictor of student success: the higher the GPA, the more likely a first-year York University student was to succeed. Existing data from OIPA showed that 26% variation in first year GPA could be explained by high school grades. Adding library usage (defined as eResource usage in this case) explained this variation by an additional 6%, so a new model that incorporates both library usage and high school grades explained variation in GPA by 32%. Library usage did not add a lot of explanatory power to the existing model, but compared to other predictors of first year academic performance it was an improvement.

There were some significant limitations to our methods, the most obvious being that the project relied heavily on units outside the library. The data could only be obtained from LCS and there were delays in getting it. The analysis relied on OIPA since they have access to student records. As a result a great deal of time was spent waiting on and following up with other campus units. The project could have been more extensive in terms of the timeframe and number of users analyzed, but the time limitations imposed by our institutional research office made it necessary to scale down the project. On the other hand our analyst at OIPA proved invaluable for his data analysis skills as well as his knowledge of predictors of academic success. Ultimately the model we used to demonstrate library impact on student success was his creation. Others who wish to replicate this project may find themselves also relying on others to obtain and analyze data, but our recommendation would be to limit any such reliance as much as possible, for example, by choosing a model that library staff can run themselves. At the very least the project team should factor possible delays into the project timeline.

The other limitation of our methods was our reliance on one measure of library usage. Reporting results to units outside the library may prove challenging if library usage is defined simply in terms of eResource usage. Other institutions replicating this project may have more ready access to other types of data (circulation, library instruction workshops, etc.), and if so we would recommend those be used. The data limitation in our case was compounded by the fact that we used EZproxy logs to measure eResource usage which meant we were in fact only measuring off-campus usage. However based on the results of our 2010 MINES survey 70% of eResource use takes place off campus anyway, so this is at least a significant data sample.[5] Another benefit of obtaining different types of library usage data is that it allows for other measures of library impact. For example, if a school tracked who uses its reference desk or library help sessions it could potentially look for the impact of those interactions on course grades or GPA.

Aside from using more data and employing different measures of library usage, there are other ways to study the impact of the library on student success through examining eResource usage and student GPA. One example would be to focus on a specific course that is known to require significant usage of eResources. One of the limitations of York's projects was that it lumped all users together. The reality is that courses in math and statistics do not rely on eResources to the extent that courses in psychology or biology do. A project team might choose to look at students enrolled in a course with a heavily weighted assignment that requires usage of databases, ejournals, etc. and then look for a correlation between use of eResources and final grades. Another idea would be to look for trends over time, assuming you can obtain historical usage data on eResources. For example, does a particular student's usage of eResources change over time and if so, is there a correlation with student success?

The major limitation to York's AiA project is that it only provides a basic correlation between library usage and student success. Despite the 6% explanatory power the EZproxy logs provided, there are too many other factors which could possibly influence a student's GPA, including discipline, class attendance, study habits, personal situation, etc. One recommendation to others wishing to replicate this study would be to hold focus groups or conduct surveys with the top students from the project's population in order to determine their best practices and perhaps the other factors contributing to their success.

York's AiA project, "Impact of Library Usage on Student Success: Exploring New Territory," can be considered a success in that it accomplished what it set out to do: quantify library contributions to student success in the institution for the very first time. However there are too many limitations on the project to create a fulsome argument for the library's actual contribution to the institution. For example, if the institution stopped funding the library would there be a drop in GPA? Hopefully though the recommendations in this chapter can provide some guidance to institutions that wish to create a stronger arguments for the value of their libraries.

Notes

1. Brian Cox and Margie Jantti, "Discovering the Impact of Library Use and Student Performance," *EDUCAUSE Review*, last modified July 18, 2012, accessed June 2, 2015, http://www.educause.edu/ero/article/discovering-impact-library-use-and-student-performance

2. Ibid.

3. Shane Nackerud, Jan Fransen, Krista Soria, Kate Peterson, Kristen Mastel and David Peterson, "Library Data and Student Success" (presentation, Library Technology Conference, St. Paul, MN, March 14–15, 2012), accessed June 2, 2015, http://digitalcommons.macalester.edu/libtech_conf/2012/sessions/28/

4. Janet Morrison, Mark Conrad, Brian Poser, Catherine Salole and Dimple Savlaet, "A Case for Change: A First Year Experience Framework at York University" (York University, 2013), 2, accessed June 2, 2015, http://www.yorku.ca/vpstdnts/initiatives/firstyearexperience/files/FYESummarySlides_CaseForChange.pdf

5. *Measuring the Impact of Network Electronic Services and the Ontario Council of University Libraries' Scholars Portal: Final Report 2011* (Washington DC: Association of Research Libraries, 2011), accessed June 2, 2015, http://www.libqual.org/documents/LibQual/publications/MINES_OCUL2011.pdf

Further Reading

Burk, Robert, Patrick Lyons, Andrea Noriega and Dragana Polovina-Vukovicet. *The Impact of Multiple Electronic Learning Resources on Student Academic Performance*. Toronto: Higher Education Quality Council of Ontario, 2013.

Nackerud, Shane, Jan Fransen, Krista Soria, Kate Peterson, Kristen Mastel and David Peterson. "Library Data and Student Success." Presentation at ARLD Day, Chanhassen, MN, March 27, 2012. Accessed June 2, 2015. http://blog.lib.umn.edu/ldss/pdf/Library%20Data%20and%20Student%20Success-ARLD20120427.pdf

Stone, Graham and Bryony Ramsden. "Library Impact Data Project: Looking for the Link between Library Usage and Student Attainment." *College & Research Libraries* 74, no. 6 (2013): 546–559.